Dearest Beloved,

This book is written for you. It's not about the book, it's about you. It is written in an easy to understand manner, with practical activations and reflections for you to find the clarity you need to arise. I pray that as you read the book, you'll find the courage to rise up into your destiny, to be the woman our loving King has designed you to be.

Love,
Ruth Saw

ARISE

AN INVITATION TO DIVINE FAVOUR
AND POWER IN TURBULENT TIMES

RUTH SAW

Published in 2021 by The Clarity Expert Publisher
Registration No.: R2020042400001
www.theclarityexpert.co

ISBN 9789811803482 (Hardback)
ISBN 9789811803475 (Paperback)
ISBN 9789811803468 (E-book)

A catalogue record for this book is available from the National Library of Singapore

I give all praise, honour and glory to my King, my Maker, my Redeemer, my Bridegroom, and the God of the Angel Armies, who helped me create and birth this book.

It is Time to Arise

And the king held out the golden scepter
toward Esther.
So Esther *arose* and stood before the king

Esther 8:4 NKJV

CONTENTS

PREFACE

Are you seeking clarity through these troubled times?

Perhaps you've sacrificed the bulk of your life for others around you, your family and your community. It's time you want to live for yourself, but you wonder what that would look like. You question what's your purpose in life and the future seems fuzzy.

Maybe on the surface, things seem to be going fine, but internally, you are struggling. You wonder in your heart, "Is this it? Is this what life is meant to be?" Recently, there has been a stirring in your heart that there is more, more to your capacity, more to your destiny. Yet you wonder, "What can I offer?" You want to find the courage for your voice to be heard, to make a difference in this world.

Or perhaps, you find opportunities ahead of you, but you refrain from them, you don't feel qualified or deem it too risky for uncertain times like these. You wish all these unpredictable times would just be over. You long for the day when you feel 100% in control or when you no longer feel like an impostor, to finally fulfil the dreams in your heart.

I want to encourage you, there is hope! AND THERE IS MORE. Perhaps, just perhaps, you are positioned in times like these, not only to find hope, but also to bring hope, not only to step into more, but also to help others step into more.

WHY THIS BOOK WAS BIRTHED

Personally, I was going through a season of stretching last year. When COVID-19 hit, my role was affected, pay was cut, but demands went higher. There were so many uncertainties that brought me a lot of anxieties.

As I was worshipping and dancing in my room, the story of the woman with the issue of blood came to mind.[1] She had sought doctors everywhere but in vain. Jesus did not even notice her in the crowd, but I admire her boldness, that she boldly came near, stretched out and touched His shawl in faith. Immediately power flowed from Jesus into the

> "Change your posture, my darling. Look up. "

---

1   Matthew 9:20–22, Mark 5:25–34, Luke 8:43–48

woman and she was healed at His feet.

She was not noticed, and possibly despised because of her condition. Yet, she stretched out in faith and found her deliverance. A hidden woman but made known to the world as an example of faith.

In response to this story, I knelt down with tears in my eyes and stretched out in faith, to touch Jesus' feet, to touch His shawl. I wanted that same power to flow through me. I felt as if there were a little tap on my shoulder, as if a voice were saying, "Daughter, look up." I felt as if someone were gently lifting my chin to look up; I felt as if I were kneeling in front of a King on a throne. I could not see His face, but I saw Him extending a scepter towards me. I felt I needed to arise from my kneeling position on the floor to stand and touch the scepter.

> Don't beg anymore, arise in My authority and walk out your dreams.

I felt as if a voice were telling me, "Change your posture, my darling. Look up. Don't beg anymore, arise in My authority and walk out your dreams. Know that you have access to Me anytime."

The same year that started out had turned out to be the best year for me. I had fulfilled my childhood dream of publishing 2 best-selling books, even though

I had failed English in school! I received unexpected opportunities to speak in large crowds and in podcasts, which was unimaginable, being an introvert! I started my own programs and clarity workshops, which helped me in my transition when I migrated back home from Sydney, Australia. Most importantly, I found likeminded friends and mentors, which I have been praying for years! They formed a family who would support me and help me grow in this journey. Thanks to COVID-19 and technology, I now have access to this family worldwide!!

> Know that you have access to Me anytime.

This is the reason why I wrote *Arise*. What was meant for evil can be turned around, despite the uncertainties. It was a personal study that became a sense of urgency to spread this good news.

I believe I have found some strategies in the book of Esther that will help you to navigate through this season. I also believe this is a time of a new era, where you can find supernatural favour in all that you do.

For some of you, you may have heard the story of Esther a gazillion times, but I encourage you to read on, because I believe there is something new, prophetically fit for this season, this new era and specifically for you. This is the time to arise in the authority of our King to receive supernatural favour and reign in life!

THIS COULD BE YOUR FINEST HOUR

In times of great shaking, it can be a time for a great awakening. The right action at the right time will bring success. With so many turbulent times and changing seasons, it is important for us to understand what to do, when to do it, even when faced with problems. Problems can unlock favour as you rise up to them, propelling you into your destiny.

Problems can unlock favour as you rise up to them, propelling you into your destiny.

Winston Churchill stepped into his role as Prime Minister during a dark season. He successfully led Britain through World War II through his inspiring speeches, and for his refusal to give in, even when things were going badly. He said this:

> *"There comes a special moment in everyone's life, a moment for which that person was born. That special opportunity, when he or she seizes it, will fulfil his or her mission - a mission for which he or she is uniquely qualified. In that moment, he or she will find greatness. It is his or her finest hour."*

Sometimes, this moment in life comes in disguise as a troubling problem. Regardless of uncertainty, regardless of the doom and gloom you may hear, this could be the greatest opportunity for a turnaround.

A shaking, a troubling time, could possibly mean a huge transfer of authority, wealth and impact, if you position yourself correctly.

I believe the moment is now.

The questions are:

At the end of this season, where will you be?

Are you positioned to attract and hold success? Are you willing to bear the temporal pain so that you not only win favour and success, but also make an impact, and leave a legacy?

The choice is yours.

Learn to seize the moment and overcome what is against you; recognise that you are uniquely positioned for the specific task you are designed for.

I pray and hope that this book, illustrated by the book of Esther from the Bible, will shed insights for you to position yourself well, no matter how painful your situation currently is.

Perhaps you started the year with depressing news, you felt like the circumstances are against you. It's not over! Have faith! Have hope! You could end your year with celebration! Let us walk this year carefully and find that access to supernatural favour.

Believe in miracles. It is time.

There is a Glory that is coming.

Be found in the glory and shine.

Come, let us arise!

YOUR BONUS GIFT

Congratulations on purchasing the book!

I wrote *Arise* for you, for it is not about the book, it is about YOU. To me, this is a movement, a call for us to gather and arise together.

Join me in the ARISE Challenge Facebook Group. There will be additional video teachings and where I will share my journey, and how you too can find the clarity to arise. It is also a platform for us to encourage each other. There is power in community. If one woman arose and saved her race, can you imagine what would happen if us ladies gather together?

You can look for the Facebook group "The ARISE Challenge" or scan the QR Code to join the group.

1

THE FORCE BEHIND THE DARKNESS

Many people struggle with the concept of a good God when the world seems to be in a mess. Why would there be sicknesses, wars and pestilences if there is a good God? How can we explain it?

There are so many parallels in the book of Esther and the gospel that could possibly explain this. In the beginning, man and woman were made in the image of God and all authority was given to them. However, the adversary came along and tricked them into handing the authority over.

God is a God of free choice. He has fully given the authority of the earth to man. What can He do if man chooses to give it away? Unfortunately, man did give it away to another god - the god of destruction, sickness and war. This explains why the world seems cursed. The world has fallen into the wrong hands. At the time of writing, there is a global pandemic that caused the world to stop. Some people say it is from God. No, it is not. It is from the other god.

In the book of Esther, the authority also landed in the hand of the adversary, Haman. The signet ring of the king was given to Haman. A signet ring represents full authority; this means Haman had full control of the kingdom, for good or bad. He can choose to destroy whomever and whenever he wishes, which was what he set out to do, to destroy all Jews in the time of the book of Esther.

> The world has fallen into the wrong hands.

Because our world is cursed by this other god, the only way to redeem it is to send another man, someone who does not originate from the first man who gave our authority away, to fight the god of this world and to redeem what was meant to be ours. That was what Jesus did. He came, born of a woman, as a son of man, to overcome the devil by what He did on the cross.

I find it a wonder to uncover so many clues about Jesus in this book! Did you know that Haman in the book of Esther was killed in the same month as Jesus on the cross? Haman died on the gallows, which in Hebrew represented "tree". Jesus too gave his life up to defeat the stronger Haman for us on a tree 2000 years ago and defeated the enemy once and for all. He has consumed all curses and has overcome. He now calls all who believes in Him, saved and free from the curse of this world. This group is now known as Christians. We bear His last name for we are His bride.

The Church is not perfect; it is made from a group of very unlikely people, seemingly very tainted at times. *God can turn all that was meant for evil to become for your good!* The Church can now be His bride because He lived up to and went beyond the vow, "Till death do us part." He rose from the dead and promised never to part from us, never to leave nor forsake us. He gave up His life so that we may receive life, and life more abundantly[2]. In this way, we can receive His purity and His wholeness, because by ourselves, we are nowhere near to God's holy standards.

Likewise, in the book of Esther, there was an unlikely marriage. Esther, a Jewish minority, a commoner, an orphan in fact, was selected to be the Queen of Persia. An unlikely covenant was made with the king. She was married to him for years, yet the authority was not with her. The signet ring was still with the adversary, Haman.

------

2 John 10:10

It appears to be a reflection of the Church today. Esther represents the Church, the bride of Christ. Though we have received the covenant with our King who died for us on the cross, some of us are not awakened to the reality that along with His finished work on the cross, came the authority to rule and reign.

The good news is the story of Esther ended in victory! God can turn all that was meant for evil to become for your good! Esther arose and petitioned to the King. The adversary Haman was slain, and the signet ring was passed to Esther and her cousin Mordecai.

It started when the story seemed to plummet into dark times, when Haman the adversary announced the annihilation of the Jews at the end of the year. It was during that dark time, that Esther found the courage to arise, to approach the king, to defeat the enemy and claim the authority back.

While the world seems to be getting darker, there is a call for Esthers and Mordecais around the world to arise. I believe the time is NOW.

So many people have said yes to Jesus but have not entered their promised land. That is the toughest place to be in, to be caught in religion and to not feel fulfilled. The key to enter the promised land is to

"Arise."

> *Then the Lord said to me, 'Arise, begin your journey before the people, that they may go in and possess the land which I swore to their fathers to give them.'*
>
> *Deuteronomy 10:11 NKJV*

Do you want to enter your promised land?

Would you arise?

In the book of Esther, the entire Jewish race in that time was saved when ONE woman chose to say yes and arose. Imagine what would happen if men and women ALL arose ?

This book is a call for us to all arise and come near to our King with boldness. It is a call for us to see that He welcomes us, and that He extends His favour towards us. It is a call for us to bring into fruition all that He has been asking us to do and have promised to give us.

> Imagine what would happen if men and women ALL arose ?

He did not die in vain. He was not flogged in vain. He did not shed his blood in vain. Ask and it shall be given unto you; seek and you shall find. God will give you immeasurably above and beyond all that you ask or think.

Let us come boldly to our King, to claim our rightful authority back to rule and reign in this life – wherever He has placed us.

It is time. His Glory is coming.

Let us arise.

2

INVISIBLE FORCE OF FAVOUR IN ESTHER

––––––––––––––––––––

The whole city rejoiced!

There was music and dancing everywhere.

What was meant to be a day of destruction turned out to be a day of celebration. Out in the public, where everyone could see, hanged on the gallows were the bodies of the enemies. The enemies were ultimately hanged on the same gallows they had created for destruction. All 10 of them, killed and then hanged. The enemies have been overthrown; they have become a public spectacle to all.

The Jews were originally despised, but now they walked with their heads held high. Fear and respect ran through the city and the cities beyond. People near and far knew that they were special, as if there were an invisible force helping them, fighting for them.

It would not have been so, if not for one woman. A simple woman, a minority, someone who was often overlooked as young or just a pretty face. Others even called her a traitor, that she concealed her own race and married for money and power. Some commented on her dressing. Regardless of gossips, of judgemental eyes, she rose up to her call, through the encouragement of her mentor, Mordecai, who supported her in this strategy to overrule the enemy. She literally saved her race, including all who ridiculed her before.

> She literally saved her race, including all who ridiculed her before.

This is the story of the book of Esther in the Bible. To some, it is a fable; to others, it is the word of God. Interestingly, the word "God" was not written in the entire story. Yet, we see His fingerprints everywhere. We find clues to Him and His supernatural favour. What we cannot argue, is that the same story seemed to be repeated in history. Could it be that the book of Esther was a prophecy of what would happen thousands of years later?

During World War II, the Nazis in Germany tried to wipe out the Jewish race too. There was great devastation and over 6 million people were killed. It was a time of doom and darkness and many lives were lost. Yet, one day, on 16 October 1945, the prominent members of the political and military leadership of Nazi Germany were hanged. Interestingly, it was also 10 of them.

Years later, regardless of being the minority, 20% of the world's Nobel Prize winners emerged from this small race. Even in the Arab-Israeli war in June 1967, despite Israel being outnumbered, they won the war in 6 days miraculously. These are a testament that there is also an Invisible Force that was helping them, fighting for them. So what can we learn from this ancient wisdom for our own lives, for our own victory?

What is this Invisible Force? How do we access this Invisible Force? What if this Invisible Force wants to help you?

Wherever you are at now, I guarantee you, there is a better future ahead of you, if you allow this Invisible Force to hold your hand and lead you through. If you find that boldness to come near to Him, you will realise that He wants to meet you. He wants you to flourish and He is doing what He can behind the scenes to

> What if this Invisible Force wants to help you?

position you, to help you. All you need to do is to arise.

This Invisible Force is actually a Person; He wants to be your King. He longs for you to draw near. Let us glean from the timeless truth of this story and learn the keys to receive supernatural favour, and to prosper, even in times of trouble.

He had already given up everything for you; what will He withhold from you?

He says, "Come."

Let us arise and come to Him.

Find the secret to partner Him, to rule and reign in this life and win.

3

PREPARATION IN MOST UNCONVENTIONAL WAYS

Do you feel that sometimes, no matter what you do, learn or grow, you feel hidden, unnoticed, or maybe unappreciated? Do you secretly believe there should be more?

Do not lose heart! This could simply be a season of hiding for your preparation for something great ahead. Even in construction, it usually takes much longer laying the foundation before the building arises and is seen!

The Bible hides secrets in names. The name Esther is derived from the Hebrew word Hester, which means "hiddenness." In Persian it means "star." While they seem to be polar opposites, the story seems to be revealing the process of transforming her from hiddenness to arising to be a star.

Isn't that beautiful? Know that what you are going through is just a season. God needs to work in you so that He can work through you. His Word promises that all these will be done![3] He did that with Esther and in due season, she arose and saved her nation. I am believing that for you too.

Esther's original name in Hebrew was Hadassah, which represents righteousness. It is derived from a Hebrew word that means myrtle. Myrtle is an evergreen plant with a pleasant fragrance. The fruit, leaves and branches are used to make medicine.

The very foundation of the process from hiddenness to arising to be a star is righteousness. On our own, we can do nothing, but we can do all things through Christ who gives us strength[4].

Esther was under the care of Hegai through the entire process. Hegai represents the guidance of the Holy Spirit; He prepares us before we meet our King. Hegai's name is so interesting! It means meditation, word, groaning and separation. In Arabic, it means burn, blaze of fire, making a murmuring noise in burning. In the Bible, there's always references to our Lord Holy Spirit as fire.

> God needs to work in you so that He can work through you.

---

3   Philippians 1:19 MSG

4   Philippians 4:13

I indeed baptize you with water unto repentance, but He who is coming after me is mightier than I, whose sandals I am not worthy to carry. He will baptize you with the Holy Spirit and fire.

Matthew 3:11 NKJV

So what process did Esther go through? She went through beauty treatments, royalty education and she learnt obedience before she was made queen.

BEAUTY TREATMENTS

When the king was looking for the next queen, he gathered beautiful young virgins and gave them twelve months of beauty treatments and preparations before they met him. Esther was one of them. She went through six months of beauty treatments with oil of myrrh, and six months with perfumes and preparations for beautifying women[5].

While it sounded good to undergo such extravagant beauty treatments, when I did the study on the words, I got a shock!! There are hidden truths that can be applied to all of us today.

---

5   Esther 2:12

1. PURIFICATION

The word for "beauty treatment" in Hebrew is "tamruq." It actually means a scraping, a rubbing. Imagine being scrapped and rubbed throughout every day for six months; it must be painful! The word actually means cleansing and purification. There is another word used for beauty treatments too; the root word is "maruq." This one is worse; it means purification too but with scouring. The difference between rubbing and scouring is that for scouring, it is rubbing with something abrasive to remove dead skin, for new growth.

The first six months, she went through scrapping and rubbing with the oil of myrrh. Oil of myrrh is a bitter oil, traditionally to embalm mummies. These treatments sound terrible, as though the cleansing and purification was a process of dying to self, so that we may live.

Why do we need to die to ourselves?

If we want to achieve anything great, we need to know this truth, IT'S NOT ABOUT YOU! It's about what God can do through you. It doesn't mean we don't dream big, but we learn to purify our motives to glorify God and not ourselves. God promises success; He wants us to be the head and not the tail. When we die to our own ambitions, it helps us to have the capacity to hold the success that God wants to pour out on us. We don't get insecure when we are tested or become proud when we succeed; we can just run our race and shine. We learn to trust God in this purification process and rid ourselves of the wrong mindsets, attitudes and habits in our lives.

> God promises success; He wants us to be the head and not the tail.

Additionally, in biblical times, myrrh incense, often in combination with frankincense, was burnt in places of worship to help purify the air and prevent the spread of contagious diseases, including those caused by bacteria. Once you are purified, it protects you from any form of contagious diseases or negative influences. This process is necessary for us to be resilient and strong.

The root word of myrrh is "marar," which means bitter. It is the same word used by Naomi when she said her life was bitter after she lost her husband and sons in Ruth 1:20. Sometimes, you may go through a season of testing and things don't make sense, just like Naomi, who experienced sudden great loss. But I want to encourage you, it's not over yet; hang on, and keep on going! Be like Naomi, return to God and watch Him bless your socks off! Naomi ended up rejoicing and became the great grandmother of King David.

Myrrh is one of the ingredients in anointing oil. Jesus Himself, when He was a child, was given myrrh, signifying the death He would have to save mankind. So know that you are not walking this season of testing alone. He has experienced all forms of emotions being rejected, being stripped, being whipped, being betrayed and misunderstood. All that we could ever experience, He had taken them to the cross.

He wore a crown of thorns so that you can wear a crown of life. His heart was pierced so that your heart can be whole. He sweat drops of blood in the garden of Gethsemane so that you can find supernatural peace. He understands you and He wants to grant you strength to walk through this season. Because He knows what is on the other side. We know He's a good God so it'll be something good. Keep on going!

2. ANOINTING

Esther went into another six months of purification again, but this time with perfumes. The word for perfumes is spices; this same word was used in the spices for the anointing oil. I believe the first part of the treatment is purification and dying to self, and the second part of the treatment is purification and anointing or supernatural empowerment.

I can imagine in the palace, people would smell Esther before they saw her, because she had been soaked in perfumes for 6 months! Our impact, our influence can be great, if we allow ourselves to go through the purification process!

There are people seeking anointing, without wanting to go through the testing process. Our God is a good God. He wants to anoint us so that we can spread His fragrance. The higher the calling, the more He wants to work in our hearts to prepare us to carry the weight of the success.

The higher the calling, the more He wants to work in our hearts to prepare us to carry the weight of the success.

There are so many examples in the Bible. David, known as the man after God's heart, was anointed at 15 years of age, but became king only at 30. But my, the things he had to go through in between! He was rejected, he was running for his life and so on. But he kept his heart pure before God. Because of that, he was able to hold his position as king for the next 40 years and the country was at peace even till the next generation.

God also seems to use those who are seemingly unqualified according to man's standards as long as they have a heart for Him.[6] David started out as a shepherd for a few sheep but ended up being the greatest king of Israel. It is not about our qualification, it's about our willing hearts.

3. REFINER'S FIRE

As we know, Hegai represented the Holy Spirit. We noted that it was because Esther found favour with Hegai that he readily gave the beauty preparations, the testing, the purification to her. She literally entered the Refiner's Fire because she found favour.

> *Now the young woman pleased him, and*
> *she obtained his favour; so he readily gave*
> *beauty preparations to her, besides her*

---

6   1 Sam 13:14

allowance.

Esther 2:9 NKJV

I do not know what you are going through now; perhaps it's a tough season or a dry season and you are wondering why. Maybe you feel there's something stirring in your heart and you sense transition is coming but you don't know what it is. You feel that you have done everything right that you know, yet all circumstances seem to be against you. Take heart! God is not against you, He is refining you; He wants you to come out of the other side stronger!

Do not entertain condemning thoughts that break you. Bring them to God; complain to God if you need to. Choose to end in praise. Bring a sacrifice of praise regardless of how you feel. He's working behind the scenes for you, even though you cannot see it.

> He's working behind the scenes for you, even though you cannot see it.

I personally went through 2 years of this season where I was travelling between Australia and Singapore for my work; I felt burnt out and isolated, and was not sure where I was going. Transition from corporate work to this coaching role was difficult. I also didn't agree with my CEO on how things were done. When I found the courage to voice out, I got knocked back many times. The company also had very high employee turnovers. There were many times I wanted to quit, but I felt that God wanted me to stay and do my best and do it unto Him. Then COVID-19 hit. After much prayer and counsel, I finally felt the green light to resign. By the grace of God, I launched my first book in 2 weeks, and it became an international best seller.

> He cares for our hearts more than what we can do for Him.

The testing seasons are only for a moment. Just when I thought the season of testing was over, another test came for me. A good one. God wanted me to stretch and step up. I feel that God stretches us in stages, and if we can persist, by His grace, He will bring us from glory to glory. We can become the person He has created us to be. I am grateful for mentors in my life who can offer me wisdom and supported me in my journey.

Jesus Himself was led by the Holy Spirit to the wilderness for 40 days of fasting and testing. He only started His powerful ministry after the season of testing. What I love about our God is that He wants our hearts to be whole and ready so that we can hold the success. He cares for our hearts more than what we can do for Him.

Esther 2:9 states that Hegai gave Esther her "allowance." The word allowance meant something properly weighed out; it is a choice portion. God will carefully weigh out the portion we need. He will not

> Stretch out in faith and come out stronger.

test us beyond what we can bear.[7] So whatever you are going through, even if you feel you can't continue, know that God knows your ability and the strength that is within you. Stretch out in faith and come out stronger.

After the women met with the king, they would return to a second house, under the custody of Shaashgaz.[8] Shaashgaz means "the servant of the beautiful" but it also means "he that presses the fleece; he that shears the sheep." One becomes beautiful as he/she is pressed, sheared.

Trust that as you walk in the midst of the fire, God will meet with you and talk with you face to face.

The Lord *talked with you* **face to face** *on*

---

7   1 Cor 10:13

8   Esther 2:14

the mountain from the midst of the fire.

Deuteronomy 5:4 NKJV

If you are going through a bitter season now, it's not over yet! Even Mordecai had to go through purification. When he heard about the Jews being annihilated, he let out a bitter cry – the word bitter is "marah," the same root word for myrrh, with which Esther had to go through for more than six months, being rubbed with the bitter oil daily. God brings each of us through these seasons not to harm us but to refine us. Like what Esther went through, it is to beautify us. Know that He will give you all you need to go through this refining fire. Through this, He will divinely lead us, stretch us and grow us into our destiny.

Both Esther and Mordecai got promoted and stood before the king at the end. Your promotion is coming. Have faith!

Trust the process, just like a caterpillar that was cooped up in a cocoon; it goes through a process where it is consumed but it transforms into a beautiful butterfly. You may feel trapped, you

> Like a caterpillar transforming into a butterfly, you don't have to crawl anymore; you can fly and go to places.

may feel life seems to be eating away, but trust the process. You will come out stronger and more beautiful! Like a caterpillar transforming into a butterfly, you don't have to crawl anymore; you can fly and go to places.

Learn to understand the season you are in and press in, steward it with His grace and know that soon, you'll be able to spread out your wings and fly.

ROYALTY EDUCATION

Although it was not written explicitly in the Bible, there are clues to the differences in lifestyle Esther would have in the city as a commoner and as a queen. These were the following that I noticed:

1. SHE LEARNT TO RECEIVE

The first obvious thing was that she was given extravagant beauty treatments a commoner would have never afforded – for free. She didn't have to pay; she didn't have to work for it. She only needed to learn to receive it so that she can come out more beautiful. How long would she have to work outside to receive one royal treatment in the palace? Esther must have been battling in her mind to receive and not reject.

Yet, she received 12 months of it! The Bible wrote that she won favour. It also wrote that she did not refuse anything that Hegai gave her. This demonstrated a beautiful balance of confidence and humility. She was humble enough to receive.

Yes, she didn't deserve it, but she received it with grace without pushing back. I feel that this is the same in our salvation story. So many people have been conditioned to the concept of religion, that one has to do something, one has to earn something before they are considered worthy. Do good, get good. Do bad, get bad. In the new age practice, they call it karma, you have to do good to get good. That could be true if we are under the god of this world.

> Gifts are meant to be free, not earned.

However, when we choose to receive what Christ has done on the cross, all the bad that we deserve has fallen on Him at the cross. This sometimes sounds too good to be true! Because of what He did, we can receive healing – spiritually, physically, emotionally and even financially. Yet, many do not reach out to receive it. It is a

> It's not about what we do; it's about us receiving His grace and extravagance.

false sense of humility to reject gifts that are poured out, when one thinks they don't deserve it. It is a form of pride! Gifts are meant to be free, not earned.

Recognise that we won't ever deserve salvation, but we can receive it in faith as His gift. It's not about what we do; it's about us receiving His grace and extravagance. This requires the renewing of the mind, that indeed, He has paid it all.

> *Bless the* Lord, *O my soul;*
> *And all that is within me, bless His holy name!*
> *Bless the* Lord, *O my soul,*
> *And forget not all His benefits:*
> *Who forgives all your iniquities,*
> *Who heals all your diseases,*
> *Who redeems your life from destruction,*
> *Who crowns you with lovingkindness and tender mercies,*
> *Who satisfies your mouth with good things,*
> *So that your youth is renewed like the eagle's.*
> *Psalm 103:1-5 NKJV*

We can choose to receive total forgiveness and live from a position of unmerited favour and abundance. We can receive His saving grace. We can receive health and supernatural youth.

2. SHE LEARNT TO DECREE

Another obvious thing was that she was given seven maids and she lived in the best place of the palace. Esther was an orphan. Even though Mordecai was looking after her, we know that Mordecai was often at the king's gate. This means before she was in the palace, she was probably almost always alone at home. She had to do everything herself. She had to rely on herself for meals, the housework, the repairs or whatever that needs to be done.

> *Then seven choice maidservants were provided for her from the king's palace, and he moved her and her maidservants to the best place in the house of the women.*
>
> *Esther 2:9b NKJV*

Suddenly, she's given not one but seven maids to look after her. The Bible also mentioned that she had eunuchs under her care too. I could imagine if she wanted a snack, she would walk to the kitchen to make it herself. Then, one of her maids would stop her and asked what she wanted. Esther had to learn to stop doing and start decreeing. Her commands set things in action. She had to learn and trust that if she says she wants food, food will be served.

We are all made in the image of God. God created the world by speaking. As a believer, we can decree and pray things into being. But sadly, most people pray after they've tried everything and got into trouble.

Imagine Esther trying to cook and the maids watching her and hoping to help but Esther kept silent. After she made a mess in the kitchen, she cried out to them for help to clean up. It would be a funny scene to watch!

Utilise what God has given you: our ability to decree and command heavenly hosts to fight for us; our ability to speak things into being. We can create by issuing decrees or we can partner with the guardian angels God sends to work with us. Yes, we all have guardian angels, whether you see them or not.

> We can create by issuing decrees or we can partner with the guardian angels God sends to work with us.

*For I can assure you that in heaven each
of their angelic guardians have instant
access to my heavenly Father.*

Matthew 18:10b TPT

They are meant to work with us to protect us and to deliver God's will.

*What role then, do the angels have? The
angels are spirit-messengers sent by God
to serve those who are going to be saved.*

Hebrews 1:14 TPT

I don't know why God wants to use us when He can do things Himself. That to me is a mystery. Even in the book of Ezekiel, He tells Ezekiel word for word exactly what to say but the bones only started moving when Ezekiel said it! That to me is mind-blowing. Why didn't God just decree it Himself? He loves us so much that He wants to partner us!

*So I **prophesied** as He commanded me,
and breath entered them, and they lived,
and stood upon their feet, an exceedingly
great army.*

Ezekiel 37:10 NKJV

I wonder if we are missing out on a lot of things in life because we just did not decree in faith. God promised that in the last days, He will pour out His Spirit on us and sons and daughters will prophesy.[9] We know His Spirit is already poured out, so now, it is our turn to prophesy and decree in faith.

There are so many Bible verses about the tongue, that death and life are in the power of the tongue.[10] Yet, it is so easy to talk about doom and gloom rather than positive things because that takes faith. It takes faith to declare, decree and trust that it will be done.

Esther managed her maids and eunuchs very well. There was such trust and bonding built among them that the sense of loyalty was so strong. First and foremost, Esther hid the fact that she was a Jew, yet she trusted the eunuch Hathach to deliver messages between her and Mordecai, which shared the secret that she was a Jew. She could entrust them with her secrets. The entire kingdom, including the King, did not know that.

> He loves us so much that He wants to partner us!

---

9   Acts 2:17

10   Proverbs 18:21

Esther also said she will fast with her maids, which I believe was remarkable. There was no record that she had Jewish maids, but the maids must have been so close to Esther that they were willing to fast, with no food and no water for 3 days! Don't forget, they still had to prepare the banquet while fasting! At this time, it is clear that Esther had gained influence and the confidence of those she led; she stepped up to her call as royalty, as a leader, by learning to delegate, to decree.

> Death and life are in the power of the tongue.

She wasn't just a pretty face! Don't ever underestimate your training ground. God will train you to lead wherever you are. For Esther, it was her maids, who were willing to risk for her. For David, it was a bunch of outcasts. For Joseph, it was a bunch of prisoners. God often tests us in the dark before He brings us to prominence. He wants to ensure our hearts can carry the weight of influence and not be proud. He wants to know that we are faithful before Him whether others can see it or not.

> Don't ever underestimate your training ground.

I want to encourage you, if you feel in some way hidden, if you feel that you've poured out so much, but nobody knows, our God knows. Be patient, promotion is coming. I declare that over your life.

Esther still needed to work hard, find wisdom and strategize but she knew she wasn't alone; having seven maids could get things done a lot faster! The Bible says we are seated with God in the heavenly realms; we are not going to be seated one day; we are seated NOW. Learn to decree like Queen Esther. Supernatural acceleration does not begin with your hands; it begins with your mouth. Do not fight as man does. Fight by speaking and ordering chaos into order. It's time to do things God's way.

> God often tests us in the dark before He brings us to prominence.

Look at the promises of God and declare your dreams to life!

Activation:

Personally, I decided to follow my heart and pursue my dream of writing even though I had failed my English and had never written a book before. I wrote down a list of declarations I

> Supernatural acceleration does not begin with your hands; it begins with your mouth.

would declare over myself every day. It was between me and God, so I could write anything I wanted, without worrying if anyone would laugh. I even boldly wrote for my first book, "I declare my book will be an international best seller." Guess what? My first book did become an international best seller, right on launch day! I was so shocked that I asked my friend to check his screen to confirm what I saw.

Psalm 139:16 NIV tells me that "all the days ordained for me were written in Your book before one of them came to be." So I trusted God that if I had that desire, He had placed it in me in the first place, as long as it is aligned to God's word. It could be written in my book in heaven. I prayed as often as I could for God to send His ministering angels to release the contents of this book to me that I would live out all that God has prepared for me.

> So I trusted God that if I had that desire, He had placed it in me in the first place.

For your activation, write down God's promises and what's in your heart and turn it into a set of declarations you can declare over yourself every day. If you have my second book, Clarity to Create, there is a free downloadable declaration template you can use for a start.

Pray this over yourself as regularly as possible:

> *Dear Heavenly Father,*
>
> *I thank You that all the days ordained for me were written in Your book. I ask that You send the ministering angels to open this book in heaven and reveal to me clarity, divine strategies and empowerment for me to make manifest ALL that You have written for my life. Grant me wisdom, divine connections and help, to step into the full destiny You have for me. I choose to step forward in faith each day.*
>
> *In Jesus' name, Amen.*

3. SHE LEARNT TO DRESS UP

Once we believe in Jesus, we are transferred to a new Kingdom of abundance. Some may still behave as if everything were scarce. We have to learn to open our eyes to heaven's resources and change our posture. Esther was not used to the jewels and the adornment, but she accepted what Hegai selected for her. She was probably comfortable in plain clothes, but she has to learn to receive adornment, precious jewels, good taste and sweet perfume.

The Bible said she had to put on her royal robes. The royal robes were designed for her, not anyone else. God has uniquely designed us to fulfil our purpose. We don't need to compare or envy; we just need to put on our royal robes where He has placed us. Take time to find the clarity of who you are and confidently step into it.

God has uniquely designed us to fulfil our purpose.

While there was not much description on how her royal robes looked like, we get some clues from Mordecai's dressing when he was promoted to royalty, that he wore a garment of fine linen.

Even the priests in the Tabernacle were instructed to wear linen. Why? It was a symbol of rest, that we are clothed with righteousness from above, that we don't have to strive to enter the Kingdom; it's not about our works, it's about His finished work.

I love the way God hides mysteries in names. Esther's name in Hebrew means hidden. This reminds me of Colossians 3:1-3 NKJV.

If then you were raised with Christ, seek those things which are above, where Christ is, sitting at the right hand of God. Set your mind on things above, not on things on the earth. For you died, and **your life is hidden with Christ** *in God.*

Colossians 3:1-3 NKJV

A lot of people find this too good to be true. This means that when God our Father looks at us, He sees perfection, not our imperfections, for we wear the robes of righteousness and are hidden with Christ in God.

Esther 2:7 KJV also describes her as "fair and beautiful." These terms were often used throughout the Song of Solomon to describe the Bride of the King, which represents the Church and all who believe in Jesus. God sees us as fair and beautiful because we are hidden in Him.

> Take time to find the clarity of who you are and confidently step into it.

Remember to actively put on these clothes. Take off all filthy clothes and put on royal robes as His Bride! See yourself beautiful!

Then, she'll probably be layered with royal silk, blue and purple sashes, jewellery and embroidered clothing. They represent royalty, His glory. It's royalty layered on righteousness. They must be heavy! Plus, with the perfume on her, people can smell her before they see her. It symbolises that God's glory on our lives can be heavy; we have to consciously put it on and to walk carefully to steward it. Walk knowing that you are causing an impact to those around you, even though you cannot see it.

> It's not about our works, it's about His finished work.

She also had to wear a crown as a queen. Do you know that when you wear a crown, you have to stand tall? You cannot slouch; you have to be upright with your head held high. Do you know that Esther cannot look down for scraps on the ground because her crown will fall? Look up! Stand tall.

> God sees us as fair and beautiful because we are hidden in Him.

Esther's crown was royal with gold and jewels. Gold represents purity. The Bible reminds us to put on the helmet of salvation, to remember

> Do you know that when you wear a crown, you have to stand tall?

His victory rather than our own worries. Someone else had carried and worn a crown of thorns so that we can wear this crown of beauty. His name is Jesus. It's time to change crowns!

I received these revelations while studying Esther. When I asked God for 5 things I can practically apply in my life, this is what I got. I pray that this blesses you!

1) SPEAK UP – Declare and decree your dreams to life.

2) LOOK UP – Look at God's unlimited abundance and help where you are called.

3) DRESS UP – Put on robes of righteousness and see yourself beautiful.

4) RISE UP – Step into the authority God has given you and fulfil your purpose.

5) STAND TALL – Know that God Almighty is backing you up and loves you 24/7.

OBEDIENCE

It was clear that Esther obtained favour in the eyes of God and man wherever she went. The word favour means grace. What was her secret?

1. SHE OBEYED THE LORD HOLY SPIRIT

Esther 2:9 said she obtained favour from Hegai. 'Obtain' in Hebrew is an active word; it means to lift, to carry or to take up. So how do we proactively pick up favour? Esther 2:15 sheds some clues: she requested nothing except what Hegai advised. In Hebrew, it meant she asked, commanded or advised nothing else. This means, she did not beg, or think she did not deserve anything else; she simply asked with certainty. She remembered she was royalty. She did not obey because she had no choice; she obeyed willingly.

She trusted Hegai would know the king a lot more. Hegai represents the Holy Spirit. We are very blessed that in the new covenant, because of the Cross, the Holy Spirit is now poured out to all men.[11] God's Word says that we are sealed with the Holy Spirit of promise, who is the guarantee of our inheritance.[12] This means that we all have Hegais in our lives who will guide us toward God's purpose for us.

---

11   Acts 2:33; Acts 10:45; Romans 5:5

12   Ephesians 1:13-14

If you have a gut feeling or intuition to do something and feel led by peace, as long as it is aligned with the Word of God, that is most probably the Holy Spirit leading you. It may still feel scary, for fear and peace can co-exist. Peace is from our Lord Holy Spirit. It is felt in the gut, our belly, for God says out of our belly will flow rivers of living water.[13] Fear is from our soul, our emotions; it is usually led by the mind. In this case, follow your heart, punch fear in the face and step forward in faith.

> Follow your heart, punch fear in the face and step forward in faith.

Allow the Holy Spirit to reveal to us what is in our King's heart and follow through. Hegai's name also sheds some light on how we can walk in the power of the Holy Spirit. It means meditation, word, groaning and separation. I believe it means that we must learn to live set-apart lives for our King, to learn to meditate on His Word and if possible, speak in the heavenly language God gifts us as a sign of our Lord Holy Spirit[14].

We find clues for obedience through Mordecai too!

---

13. John 7:38 KJV
14. Acts 2:4, Romans 8:26

Mordecai was the son of Jair and son of Shimei. Jair means "He enlightens," or "One giving light." I believe that represents our Lord. The root word of Shimei in Hebrew is "shama," which actually means "hear and obey"! It was the same word when Solomon asked God for wisdom, for a discerning or 'hearing' heart. 'Hearing' includes obeying!

Obeying our Lord Holy Spirit brings us discernment and wisdom. It is greater than just knowledge. Wisdom is knowledge applied. We can't gain wisdom if we don't apply what we know!

Isn't it amazing how God hides so many secrets in names?

Activation:

Meditate on Psalm 23, one verse per day.

If you need, you can refer to my YouTube channel (Ruth Saw – Clarity Expert) under the playlist "Meditation Fire" where I've created videos on word-for-word reading of God's Word.

2. PARTIAL OBEDIENCE IS NOT OBEDIENCE!

There is one thing we must remember about obedience. Partial obedience is considered as disobedience!

The Jews had to face this trouble of annihilation because of a partial obedience that happened generations ago. Haman, the adversary, was the son of an Agagite. This was repeated throughout the book of Esther, so it needs attention.

> Partial obedience is considered as disobedience!

Agagites were the descendants of the Amalekites whom God instructed King Saul to destroy completely about 550 years ago.[15] Amalek represents atheism or rejection of God. King Saul won the war; sadly, he didn't kill them completely as God commanded. Because of that, he was rejected as king. God considered that Saul did not carry out His instructions, even though King Saul partially obeyed.[16]

This explains why Esther had to go through such long extensive beauty treatments-a purification process. It is for our protection. God wants to rid everything that stands in the way completely, for a completely

---

15   1 Sam 15:3

16   1 Sam 15:10

yielded heart to fully obey, so that God can readily pour out blessings and success in our lives.

Our God is not an autocratic God. He gives us free choice but gently guides us for our good, so that we can possess the good land He has for us.[17]

3. SHE OBEYED HER MENTOR

Esther was brought into the palace and into royalty. Yet, she did not become proud and remained accountable to Mordecai. Esther was the daughter of Mordecai's uncle. She was orphaned at a young age and Mordecai took her as his own and looked after her. Even when Esther became queen, Mordecai would very often pace in front of Esther's palace. They remained in contact, close proximity and relationship, and helped each other. They communicated well for the things to be done. She also submitted to his authority. When he told her not to reveal that she was a Jew, she didn't.

She was open to rebuke and instructions from Mordecai. She was moved to a place of higher visibility, the best place in the harem, and then she became Queen, yet she remained coachable and did

---

17   Deuteronomy 6:18

not become proud. That was the key to her success.

Reflection:

Ask yourself, who are the Mordecais, the mentors in your life?

4

A CALL TO ARISE

The book of Esther is one of the two books in the bible where God was not mentioned. So many of us have been waiting for an audible call of God, but the book of Esther reminds us that God has positioned us where we are for a time like this. Promotion comes from the Lord. Both Mordecai and Esther stepped into their purpose and calling by responding and doing what is right, not because of an audible voice.

1. WE ARE ALREADY CALLED

He has already called you. Recognise that He has placed you where you are for a purpose.

This is possibly one of the most relevant books as we seek out our calling in the different spheres of our lives. For too long, Christians have placed ministry work on a pedestal, neglecting the meaning and purpose where God has placed them for the bulk of the week. It can become a form of ministry idolatry if one values the service in church as more important than the time to excel in our respective posts – be it at home or in the office or business. But the book of Esther reminds us that God has placed us in our respective assignments to glorify Him. That's where we spend most of our time, so surely He has ordered our steps, to represent Him there. He will give us levels of authority where we can be of great influence for the glory of His name.

You will also find that God speaks to everyone, Christians and non-Christians, to fulfil His calling. You don't have to see God only in church. The purpose of church is to be of influence to the world, not just to the Christians. See God bigger and see Him so actively guiding you even in your work or seemingly mundane activities.

Mordecai reminded Esther to look at how God has placed her there. She has received so much supernatural favour to be queen; surely, she can see God's divine leading. Sometimes we don't need an audible voice; God may call us through people around us or through the pressing need based on our position. Sometimes He positions mentors in our lives to advise us.

Imagine Esther rejecting Mordecai's advice, saying she needs to hear an audible voice of God. What would happen? If we were to open our eyes to see where God has placed us, maybe it is sufficient to move forward. That takes faith. I don't mean to do things recklessly; that's why it's good to surround ourselves with mentors and friends who love Jesus. More often than not, God speaks to our hearts. Leaders move forward despite the moments of hesitation, despite the sacrifice.

> Leaders move forward despite the moments of hesitation, despite the sacrifice.

Perhaps you feel that there is something more to your life, but you feel caught up in boring and daily routines. Esther had daily boring routines for 5 years before she arose to the king. God is always working behind the scenes.

You may feel that there's nothing you can do, you are not sure what's ahead or maybe you are currently burdened by supporting your family. Ruth felt that way when she was widowed, and she didn't even know what was next. All she knew was to do her best at where she was. She took care of her mother-in-law, she did her best to glean left-over wheat, and worked from day to night. She did her best in her position and God promoted her[18]. How can you be more effective where God has placed you? How can you work and take care of your family at the same time? Are there areas you can find the courage to step up or speak up? Who can you bless?

> God is always working behind the scenes.

Do not feel discouraged with routines; trust God to promote you. Do not reject opportunities that come your way; trust God to grace you. My mentor shared with me once, that if a door opens in front of you, God probably allowed it, so step into it and allow Him to stretch you. Find the courage to step up.

> Never underestimate what He can do in your life.

We are all called to full-time ministry, for we are all married to our King.

---

18   Ruth 1-4

We bear His name wherever He has placed us.

Never underestimate what He can do in your life.

2. LISTEN TO YOUR TRUE HEART

When there is a major decision in your life, learn from Esther how she made her decisions. Esther felt that she has not been called by the king so she hesitated, but Mordecai reminded her and asked her not to "think in her heart" that she would be safe.

The word heart in Hebrew means the soul, which includes the emotions she may face, e.g. fear. Her initial decision was led by the soul – her emotions, possibly fear, the fact that the king had not called her. But don't forget, she was still in the position. So listen to Mordecai's advice: don't look at how you feel; look at the position God has given you.

> Don't look at how you feel; look at the position God has given you.

When you find yourself making decisions based on your soul or emotions, it is time to check in with God and ask Him to illuminate your true heart, your inner man. The word heart used in the verse below is a different word in Hebrew; it represents the will, the inner man.

> *Search me, O God, and know my **heart**;*
> *Try me, and know my anxieties; And see*
> *if there is any wicked way in me and lead*
> *me in the way everlasting.*

Psalm 139:23-24 NKJV

Have you wanted to do something but decided not to, because of fear? Your initial desire to want to do it, that's your will, your inner man, i.e. your true heart. The fear you feel is from another source, from your soul, your emotions. Understanding the difference helps you to make decisions based on your inner man and step into your destiny. The Bible clearly says how the desires of your heart (your inner man) can be met.

> *Delight yourself also in the* Lord, *and He*
> *shall give you the desires of your heart.*
> *Commit your way to the* Lord, *Trust also*
> *in Him, ...*

Psalm 37:4-5a NKJV

When you are at the crossroads of making decisions, take time off, hang out with Jesus (not religion), think about your past successes with your King and bear out your inner heart desires to Him.

Then, take action! Ask God to show you the how, sometimes, He may just show the first step. It's ok! Commit to walk in it despite the fears you feel and trust Him!

3. FACE YOUR FEARS AND WIN

Esther deliberated in her heart, her inner man, and stepped into it by faith. She was ready to pay the price; she said, "If I perish, I perish." She faced the very thing she feared. She committed her ways to the LORD and trusted Him. Sometimes, the decisions we make may not seem logical, but if we would choose to listen deeper to our inner man, if we were to confront our fears, we can possibly make the best decisions for our lives.

> By fulfilling your dreams, you free others to fulfil theirs also!

The word "courage" comes from a French word that means heart. Taking advantage of an opportunity at the right time requires a big heart. Courage comes when your heart is enlarged for others. Imagine the people you will impact and influence if you choose to face your fears. By fulfilling your dreams, you free others to fulfil theirs also! Jesus too rose up for us, to pay our sins on the cross for us; He considered it a joy set before Him to have endured the cross.

Some of us live lives so that we can escape the terrors and fears, but sadly if we do, we probably have not risen up to all that God has given us. Esther could have chosen to be silent and maybe she could live a comfortable life as a queen, but she will never realise the reason why God placed her there. Don't look at the circumstances; look at your position and what you can do. If He had planned for you to be there, there must be a reason behind it!

Mordecai mentioned to Esther, if she doesn't do it, deliverance will arise elsewhere. The word "arise" means to take a stand. Whatever situation you are faced with, ask yourself, where are you going to take the stand? In your own safety or stand on the side of God? Which one has a better chance of winning?

He is looking at the posture of the heart.

The good news is, Esther didn't die, she arose and saved the nation. That's how good our God is. He is looking at the posture of the heart. Yes, there may be some very trying situations we have to go through;

it becomes a season of stretching and growth. When Esther saw the worst, she went ahead anyway. She wasn't confident of her task at all, yet she was willing to step in because she realised she was in a position to do so.

Esther willed her heart to arise; she saw greatness on the other side. If we realise what we can do in our position, but choose to play it safe, we'll end up only getting by. In the end, we might be taking the bigger risk of never stepping into our destiny! Think long term.

Ask God to help you in your decisions. Sometimes, the window of opportunity is only for a season; don't tarry for too long!

The beautiful part of this journey of facing your fears is that when you come out on the other side, you will know that He's got your back! He will deliver you as you commit your next step to Him.

I pray that as you read on, you'll begin to discover your calling and more importantly, your assignment for such a time as this.

When to you arise?

The time is now, yes, NOW, in turbulent times.

He Himself will lead us to our paths, for His name's sake!

Go in the might of yours, in the midst of troubles, and find victory.

Reflections:

Ask God for understanding in your position now.

Who are the mentors you can seek counsel from?

Do you need to make certain decisions? Sit down and look at God's favour in your life and in your position till now. Thank Him. Re-read Ps 139:23-24 and Ps 34:7. Then, hang out with Jesus and ask Him to search your heart and to show you your inner heart desires. Put your emotions at His feet. Make that decision in faith. Then, don't look back.

It is a call to arise, to stand up, to find the boldness to speak up and make a difference. It reminds us that in the face of evil arising, we too can arise by positioning ourselves through prayer, fasting and uniting together as one, not just in the Church, but in the marketplace and in different spheres of life. When evil arises, the Church has to arise and claim the victory.

> It is a call to arise, to stand up, to find the boldness to speak up and make a difference.

What are the communities you can plug into for strength and support to go through this journey? Take time to build and invest in the relationships and learnings. Get a prayer partner if you can.

5

THE ENEMY'S STRATEGIES

God works in ways that are supernaturally natural. So does the enemy. This chapter reveals the common strategies that the enemy uses, often in disguise. If we understand the tactics that he uses, then it is easier for us to recognise when he is in action and what we need to do.

1. CURSE AND COMMAND

Haman had the signet ring. Whatever he wrote became the decree of the land. It was as if the king wrote it. The king, to a certain extent, had limited control as the authority had landed in the adversary's hands.

> God has placed you in your assignment for a reason!

What kind of decree did he write? In the book of Esther, he wrote death. He decreed that they will all soon die. Likewise, the god of this world wrote death, death in many forms: in disasters, in wars, in sicknesses, and through all forms of perversion and injustice.

That's why we need Jesus, for He has borne all the curses and He gives us new life. He wants to give us life, and life more abundantly. Be bold to take up your authority and pray for miracles, such as for healing. If we recognise that we are no longer under the curse of this world, then we can walk in greater freedom, even if things are against us now.

> "Let us stop speculating when Jesus is returning to earth but rather, let us OCCUPY the seven mountains."

The god of this world often uses authority to enforce his works, to enforce his curse in all different spheres of influence, such as gender inequality, racism, corruption, etc. There are seven mountains of influence as mentioned by Johnny Enlow in https://restore7.org/. They are Religion (Church), Government, Economy, Family, Education, Media, and Arts & Entertainment.

The Church is only one of the seven mountains! God has placed you in your assignment for a reason! I love what Johnny said in one of his messages; he said, "Let us stop speculating when Jesus is returning to earth but rather, let us OCCUPY the seven mountains." How true!

How do we occupy these mountains? We need individuals like you to rise up like Esther, Mordecai, as well as other heroes of the Bible and of modern times in these respective spheres, to rise to the top and/or to voice out against unjust activities. Never underestimate where God has placed you; you are positioned to bring His light, to actually move and change things and turn things around, regardless of how dim the news can be.

For example, I have a friend, whom God led to a job in an industry which she was initially not open to. But the string of events revealed God's hand and favour on it, so she at least was open to go try it out. It was in the gaming industry. When she went to the interview, she was surprised that believers do occupy some of these roles in this sector, even at the top management! In addition, those who were there, embraced godly values and desired to make a difference through their influence in setting policies to protect the public.

If we become overly legalistic and avoid such controversial sectors, then guess who is occupying the top in these sectors? Which is worse? Who will protect the people? That is an example of occupying a mountain of influence.

I pray that we have godly people with godly principles at the top of all sectors, including the seemingly controversial sectors such as arts & entertainment or media. Esther herself arose in Persia, outside her race and culture, and saved her race. God placed Daniel in the Babylonian kingdom for many years, so why would He not do likewise now? If God had not given closed doors for a long time to my friend and worked in her heart before this favourably popped up, she would not have been open to the interview in the first place. She knows it is God who has positioned her there. She found newfound purpose in her role.

> Know that God is working behind the scenes even if you don't hear his audible voice.

Know that God is working behind the scenes even if you don't hear his audible voice. Remember it was God's supernatural favour that Esther became queen. If such opportunity opens for you, step into it; do not discount yourself. Away with the impostor syndrome! Impostor syndrome refers to an internal experience of believing that you are not as competent as others perceive you to be. Impostor syndrome happens when we look at ourselves too much. Look to God. Remember, it's not about you! Trust God to stretch you for the role. Esther was an orphan, she did not disqualify herself, but she stepped into her role as queen.

> Trust God to stretch you for the role.

There was evidence of His supernatural favour for Mordecai too. The book of Esther records that one day, the king could not sleep, so he asked to read the book of Chronicles and he realised that Mordecai had once saved his life. It prompted him to honour Mordecai, exactly on the day when Haman wanted to come and ask the king to kill Mordecai. God speaks to all; sometimes He puts things in our path right when necessary. Even if it means waking someone up in the middle of the night! He orchestrates all events and people for the good of those who love Him. God may seem silent, but He always shows up at the right place, when one chooses to arise, at the right time.

> God is never late; He is at work way before we realise!

He is a God of providence; He already knew all these would take place, and dethroned Queen Vashti nine years before this edict was sent, so that Esther could be queen five years before the edict. God is never late; He is at work way before we realise!

2. CONDEMNATION

Haman constructed the gallows. He wanted Mordecai and others to visibly see the consequences of going against him. The gallows constructed was 50 cubits high, which is around 23 metres or 7 storeys high. This is almost as high as the walls of the palace! He did not need such high gallows to hang a person. Why did he spend all the effort and money to create such a tall gallows?

I believe this was such that wherever you were in the city, you could see it. It created fear and reminded people of the consequences they would have in disobedience.

Satan's strategies have not changed. He uses legalism and religion to sometimes create condemnation in your hearts. He uses your logical mind to trick you, e.g., "Oh, I have done something bad; I deserve something bad." This repels you from coming to God. You wonder, "Why should I? I'm already stained; I'm so lousy; I'm not good enough."

That is a lie from the pit of hell!!

> *There is therefore now no condemnation to those who are in Christ Jesus, who do not walk according to the flesh, but according to the Spirit.*
>
> Romans 8:1 NKJV

Whenever such condemning thoughts come to you, regardless of the mistakes you've made, can I encourage you to look at who was hung at the gallows? It was Haman!

The root word for "gallows" is "tree."

2000 years ago, a stronger Haman, the god of this world, was also conquered when Jesus was hanged on the tree. He died in our place, so that we can go free. That is our salvation story. Haman died in Nissan, the same month when Jesus died. It's symbolic that Jesus defeated the enemy on the cross once and for all for the human race!

God wants you to have abundant life.

Come to the other gallows; see His blood poured out to redeem you, receive His forgiveness and find the strength to walk free. It may take a while but as you keep looking at where your sins have been duly paid, it will transform you from the inside out.

> *Christ has redeemed us from the curse of the law, having become a curse for us (for it is written, "Cursed is everyone who hangs on a tree"), ...*

Galatians 3:13 NKJV

God wants you to have abundant life. He wants to bring heaven on earth for you. Now it's all been made possible. That is our Jesus! He was the first one who arose and defeated the greater Haman by sacrificing His life – for you and me.

3. CONFUSION

When Haman issued the edict to annihilate all Jews and to plunder their possessions, the city of Shushan became perplexed. Whenever the enemy is at work, it leads to people feeling confused and at times sorry for themselves. Have you felt like this before? Have you wondered why life seems unfair and why God seems silent?

All the Jews started mourning, weeping and wailing. They lay in sackcloth and ashes. Their spirit died. Mordecai mourned, but only for a season. Instead of asking, "Why?" He asked, "What can we do to solve this matter?" and "Who is able to do it?" He asked Esther to arise and speak to the king.

It is okay to weep for a season; we can't deny how we feel. But there comes a point we need to ask ourselves, "What can I do to move forward?" and take the next step. God's Word is a lamp to our feet and as we step forward in faith, our path will be illuminated. Find the courage within to speak up, to step up, to walk away, to forgive, to reconcile... and so on, whatever you feel led to do in your situation.

> God's Word is a lamp to our feet and as we step forward in faith, our path will be illuminated.

Or perhaps you feel you've been overlooked in the workplace. You have worked so hard but you have not been noticed. Mordecai must have felt that too. He helped save the king's life, but he was not rewarded straightaway. It was only months later, at the most suitable time, when Haman wanted to kill Mordecai, that the king suddenly remembered about Mordecai's accomplishment and rewarded him. God orchestrates

> God orchestrates everything in time for our benefit and protection. Trust Him!

everything in time for our benefit and protection. Trust Him!

TEN SONS OF HAMAN

Haman was hanged on the gallows the day Esther petitioned to the King. All of Haman's inheritance was then given to Esther and Mordecai. But Haman's ten sons were killed and hanged only eleven months after Haman had died! This means the gallows remained there. But the tables have turned! The gallows no longer triggered fear in Mordecai as Haman was dead; it became a reminder that all their enemies would die there!

I believe that this represents the journey a believer has to go through. At the time of receiving Christ as our Saviour and King, we receive the full righteousness paid to us on the cross. Spiritual death has been defeated at the cross. However, our soul, our nature needs to be slowly transformed by the renewing of our minds. We must actively eliminate any wrong beliefs or attitudes and have our hearts healed to wholeness.

It is sad that a lot of Christians are still living defeated lives, because they haven't taken authority and rid themselves of 'the ten sons' and find full victory. What was interesting is that all ten sons of Haman have a reference to self in their names. It appears that this is a journey of dying to self, so that we may truly live. The call to die to self is a paradox, for when we die to self, we enter into wide-open spaces[19], so that we may live an abundant life.

> We must actively eliminate any wrong beliefs or attitudes and have our hearts healed to wholeness.

Eradicating them is so important that Esther had them killed and then hanged for the world to see. Let that be a visible reminder to not entertain such thoughts and attitudes any longer.

There are various interpretations of the names of Haman's 10 sons. For the ability for us to practically apply this in our lives, the meanings of these names were adapted from the book, *The Psychology Of God – The Ten Sons Of Haman*, written by L.M. McCormick. L.M. McCormick is an author in the United States and holds a degree in Psychology and a Masters in Communication.

---

19. Psalm 18:19 CEB

Please note that some of the names and content was also modified; as far as possible, New Testament examples or illustrations were used.

No.	Name	Meaning	Nickname
1	Parshandatha	Curious Self	The Busy Body
2	Dalphon	Weeping Self	The Pity Party
3	Aspatha	Sufficient Self	The Orphan
4	Poratha	Indulgent Self	The Party Animal
5	Adalia	Weak Self	The Inferior One
6	Aridatha	Assertive Self	The Bully
7	Parmashta	Preeminent/Inflated Self	The Narcissist
8	Arisal	Imprudent Self	The Striving One
9	Aridal	Prideful Self	The Arrogant One
10	Vaizatha	Righteous Self	The Legalistic One

1. THE FIRST SON: THE BUSY BODY

The first son's name was Parshandatha, which means the "Curious Self", or "I am Curious." When we use this trait to poke into other people's affairs, it is like gossip or judgement of others. That is very unhealthy for the soul.

The words of a gossip merely reveal the wounds of his own soul, and his slander penetrates into the innermost being.

Proverbs 18:8 TPT

Gossips not only reveal their own wounds, but also have the ability to hurt others deeply. If we look at the original definition of innermost being, it means innermost soul. Nothing can wound the soul so deeply like gossip. Don't do that; don't even participate in it! Remember we are royalty, so let us rise higher and only let good things out of our mouths.

Some people choose to gossip about others on the pretext, "I'm sharing with you so we can pray." Be wise and learn to judge the spirit behind the person who is saying it.

When we project our curiosity on ideas or others, they can form distractions to steer us off our paths. Such distractions can be running after the next shiny object or other experiences that causes some form of addiction or reliance. Many of these distractions begin with an innocent-sounding "I wonder if..." and lead a person down a road of earthly creations that goes into everything from addictions to substance abuse, sexual practices to spiritual influences. The easiest way to test is to look at the fruit: do you feel continual peace and freedom, or does it bind you and cause you to be addicted to these experiences? All distractions and addictions hinder us from intimacy with God and trusting Him.

Antidote: Impart Grace

If you find yourself caught up in discussions or gossip, or always looking for the next shiny object and getting distracted, know that God has placed in you an ability to connect with people and an ability to learn and grow. Use these abilities wisely, by imparting grace to all around you. Save the time used for gossip to be curious about learning to improve yourself and start bearing fruit. See the impact that you will make on others and also on your life as you grow.

> Remember we are royalty, so let us rise higher and only let good things out of our mouths.

Remember that you carry grace to others and yourself. If you want to judge, judge your own words and actions! Do not participate in gossip; do not even listen to them. Our role is to impart grace to others through our words.

> Our role is to impart grace to others through our words.

Activation:

Meditate on the following verses and pray about them regularly.

> *Let no corrupt word proceed out of your mouth, but what is good for necessary edification, that it may impart grace to the hearers.*
>
> Ephesians 4:29 NKJV

> *Let the words of my mouth and the meditation of my heart, Be acceptable in Your sight, O Lord, my strength and my Redeemer.*
>
> Psalms 19:14 NKJV

2. THE SECOND SON: THE PITY PARTY

The second son of Haman was named Dalphon, which means "Weeping Self" or "Self-Pity." The dictionary defines self-pity as dwelling on your own sorrows or misfortune. Basically, this person forgets to be thankful in all circumstances[20] and to trust that God

---

20   1 Thessalonians 5:18

will work out all things for our good.[21]

Life happens and sometimes it can be tough. I'm not discounting the things you may have to go through, the losses and the injustices you may suffered. There is a season for mourning, but the good news is, God meets us at where we are, and He wants to take us out.

Having a victim mentality, a feeling of "everyone is against me" or "woe to me" can get you the attention you desire, but it will not help you get out of the situation. We can't hang around there for too long!

Hellen Keller lost her sight and hearing when she was 19 months old. Yet, she became the first deafblind person to earn a Bachelor of Arts degree. She also wrote 14 books! This is what she said:

> *Self-pity is our worst enemy and if we yield to it, we can never do anything wise in this world.*
>
> *Helen Keller (1880 – 1968)*

There is a story of how Jesus healed the man of the tombs in Mark 5:1-20. There was a man who hung

---

21   Rom 8:28

around the tombs night and day. He would cry out and cut himself with stones. It's a reflection of self-pity and camping around previous disappointments or losses, represented by the tombs. What is interesting is that this man was possessed not by one spirit but by a legion. There were so many of them, such that they entered a herd of 2000 pigs! Please don't camp around the tombs for too long!

After Jesus healed him, he no longer spent his time around the tombs, but went around sharing God's love to others. Katie Souza, who specialises in healing of the soul, shared in her teaching, that this man ended up clothed and in his right mind, sitting next to Jesus. The word "clothed" means "mantled". When he was healed, he stepped out of the tombs, he was mantled and gifted from above with an anointing to be of influence. The story ended with the people in the city being amazed. He physically wore new clothes, found new friends and changed locations from tombs to the city.

Antidote: Get out of the tombs!

If you find yourself hurt and disappointed in the past, and constantly talking about your sorrows, God can turn your mess into a powerful message. If you choose to step out of the tombs and sit by Jesus' feet, watch Him anoint you from on high, with a supernatural power, a supernatural mantle that will enable you to be effective and be of influence. It can be a painful journey, but it's time and it's worth it! Let Jesus help you!

The man changed locations. I feel that metaphorically we need to invite God to the tombs and help us change our perspective. It doesn't mean that we run away from our current circumstances, but it does mean a change in perspective since God is in it. Ask God for a new perspective so that you can get out of this pity party in your soul. For example, do you find it hard to forgive? Take responsibility not to hang around the tombs, the losses, and move forward. The good news is that you don't have to do it alone. Jesus wants to help you. Yield to Jesus and let Him forgive through you. Ask God what you can learn from the situation and for wisdom on what to do next, then move ahead.

> God can turn your mess into a powerful message.

I firmly believe, if we yield to Jesus, God can turn our biggest pain into a wonderful testimony and influence, just like the man from the tombs!

Activation:

What can you actively do to get out of the tombs?

Think of something practical and you can apply straight away, for example, changing your language.

3. THE THIRD SON: THE ORPHAN

The third son of Haman was named Aspatha, which means "self-sufficient" or "assembled self." This person wants to be in control and be self-reliant. He or she can be someone very capable but very often feels the entire weight on his or her shoulders.

Overly self-sufficient people also tend to not seek help or deny help from the people around them, maybe because they want to be in control or maybe they fear rejection. It can also make them isolate themselves or focus on tasks instead of the people around them. We need a healthy balance of being self-sufficient and learning to receive help.

This is no small matter. There had been studies that linked youths not seeking help before suicides to their perception that they should solve problems on their own. [22]

Even Jesus Himself, Son of God, Son of Man, never did anything alone. He often had at least Peter, James and John when He performed the miracles. When He was very stressed and praying with sweat like drops of blood in the garden of Gethsemane, He still wasn't alone. We see in His prayer He was speaking to His Father.

The Bible sometimes can seem to be contradictory. It says apart from Jesus we can do nothing, yet another verse says I can do all things through Christ who strengthens me. What does it mean?

> *"I am the vine; you are the branches. If you remain in Me, and I in you, you will bear much fruit; apart from Me you can do nothing.*
>
> *John 15:5 NIV*
>
> *I can do all things through Christ who*

---

22   Labouliere CD, Kleinman M, Gould MS. When self-reliance is not safe: associations between reduced help-seeking and subsequent mental health symptoms in suicidal adolescents. Int J Environ Res Public Health. 2015 Apr 1;12(4):3741-55. doi: 10.3390/ijerph120403741. PMID: 25837350; PMCID: PMC4410213.

strengthens me.

Philippians 4:13 NKJV

I believe it means that you don't have to carry all your burdens on your own. Carry them through Christ who will strengthen you. You don't need to strive on your own, but with Him, you can do impossible things and still find supernatural favour and ease. Pass that burden to Him to do it through you. With what Jesus has done on the Cross, we now have the Father, Jesus and our Lord Holy Spirit all on our side. Know that They love you and They want to help you. Feel free to come to Them at all times.

Everyone hears the famous verse "I can do all things through Christ who strengthens me." What is interesting is that we know Paul was a capable man, but he continued in next verse addressing those he was writing to, that they have shared in his distress. Even in Paul's own journey, he never did anything alone without community.

Antidote: Find your community & commune with your King

If you find yourself constantly on your own and carrying your burden alone, know that God has placed in you a strong resilience and strength. Imagine how this can be multiplied and extended when you gather together in a community. One man can chase a thousand; two men can put ten thousand to flight. Imagine the multiplication when you choose to connect. It may feel that you are taking a step back, slowing down for others, but trust that God is knitting you to a web and army of people so that together, you can come out stronger.

> You don't have to carry all your burdens on your own.

I write with my personal experience; I know it can be difficult to find a group who can understand you and support you. Pray and ask God for it; it may take some time for you to build relationships, but it will come. It took a long while for me, but praise God, I finally found my family! It was only after I found my family that God

> He wants you anchored and supported, before He launches you into your destiny.

launched me into my ministry. Don't underestimate the power of community. Sometimes, God wants you to find your tribe first; He wants you anchored and supported, before He launches you into your destiny.

I don't know what you are going through. Be mindful who you share this with; find a group of people who can support you and pray along with you. If it is a season where you still need time to build relationships, remember

> One man can chase a thousand; two men can put ten thousand to flight.

you can place your burdens at King Jesus' feet and that your Heavenly Father wants to minister to you and give you the peace and strength you need. Ask our Lord Holy Spirit to help you tangibly feel God's presence. One touch from God can take away years of stress!

Activation:

Which community can help you to grow? Take time to invest in these relationships.

How do you see your Father in Heaven? Ask Him to meet you where you are.

Take time to cast your cares unto King Jesus.

Meditate on John 7:38 KJV. Close your eyes, ask our Lord Holy Spirit for a tangible presence of God's peace and start to feel that river of peace gushing out from your belly.

4. THE FOURTH SON: THE PARTY ANIMAL

Poratha, the name of the fourth son of Haman means "self-indulgent." Interestingly, the Hebrew meaning of the name also means "fruitful." This means that this person can be successful and fruitful, but the attention was spent on self-gratification rather than on others.

Genesis 12:3 reminds us that God has blessed us so that we can be a blessing to others. It doesn't mean that we don't get to enjoy the finer things in life, but it does mean that we are called to bless others along this journey too.

Being overtly self-indulgent can blind us and turn us away from God and long life too. Solomon was known as the wisest king; he wrote in Ecclesiastes he did not withhold himself from all that he desired; that included 1000 wives and concubines!! He ended up dying before his time and being swayed by different forms of idolatry. Even the wisest king can fall through self-indulgence!

What I find interesting is that self-indulgent people can often be the ones who criticise others of being indulgent, especially to God. Judas, who betrayed Jesus for 30 pieces of silver for himself, criticised Mary for extravagantly pouring the jar of perfume on Jesus.

The beauty and grace of God is that even if one is self-indulgent, God's mercy and grace will always be there. It is just that the person has to learn the hard way! We remember the parable of the prodigal son, who requested his father to split his inheritance and squandered away all his money. He came to a point where food for the pigs looked better than his, before he returned to his father.

The benevolence of God is that as a Father, He always welcomes us back with wide open arms. He is constantly checking and waiting for His sons and daughters to return. That's our Father!

My encouragement is: why go through the hard way? Abandon self-indulgence and come to His throne straightaway!

Antidote: Seek to bless our King and others

If you find yourself blessed and are fruitful, congratulations! Allow God to multiply your gifts and what you have in your hands as you choose to bless Him and others. Let Him touch your heart and give you a deeper meaning, a purpose for your capability that truly satisfies. Let Him refresh you like no other substance or experience can.

> Let Him refresh you like no other substance or experience can.

Mary didn't know much. She was not eloquent, but she was extravagant with our Lord Jesus. Her story was mentioned in all 4 gospels. Take time to be extravagant in worship; seek to bless our King. When you are thankful for Him and His grace, He will turn your heart towards others, such that you'll find deep joy in blessing others.

Activation:

Worship our King!

It is proven that people are happier when they give! God's Word holds true! It is more blessed to give than to receive. He who refreshes others will himself be refreshed.

Take time to think about whom you can bless today –
in word, in deed or financially. You may want to write
a note of encouragement.

> He who refreshes others will himself be refreshed.

You may want to sow a seed into a particular ministry or charity.

5. THE FIFTH SON: THE INFERIOR ONE

The fifth son of Haman is Adalia, which means "weak self." It could mean false humbleness or inferiority complex, both of which are not from God.

This person also gets very sensitive to people's remarks or is emotionally affected by what others say. In psychology, an inferiority complex is an intense personal feeling of inadequacy, often resulting in the belief that one is in some way deficient, or inferior, to others. Because of that, they don't expect much, and they don't accomplish much. It generally stems from comparison with others, which ironically originates from pride. It is not having the clarity of who they are. God said we are fearfully and wonderfully made. If God says so, who are we to say otherwise? When we feel inferior, we are telling God He didn't do a good job.

The clearest example is the Exodus story. God performed miracles, including the parting of the Red Sea for the group of people to walk over. Surely, by then, they would have known that the God who controlled everything, including the sea, was on their side. Yet, the first generation died in the wilderness, never making it to the promised land. That's because they were looking to themselves

> When we feel inferior, we are telling God He didn't do a good job.

and comparing themselves with the enemies they had to fight. They forgot that the King of Kings was on their side. They forgot the same God who parted the Red Sea, the same God who fed them with manna from heaven, would fight for them. They didn't expect much, so they didn't accomplish much. They wandered in the wilderness and sadly, never stepped into their promised land.

God has so much in store! He is saying, "Come take it; I will grant you victory." Maybe it is time to stop wondering and literally lift your eyes off your own weak self and look to the Strong One who fights for you.

Remember His grace.

And He said to me, "My grace is sufficient for you, for My strength is made perfect in weakness." Therefore most gladly I will rather boast in my infirmities, that the power of Christ may rest upon me.

2 Corinthians 12:9 NKJV

God is not looking for perfect people. He is looking for people who will put their faith in Him who is God Almighty. Yes, we acknowledge our weaknesses, yet we rejoice that He will use us to display His glory. Then we step out in faith and obedience to all that He has for us.

But God has chosen the foolish things of the world to put to shame the wise, and God has chosen the weak things of the world to put to shame the things which are mighty; ...

1 Corinthians 1:27 NKJV

It does not mean we do not work hard to improve ourselves and be a master at what we do. But never despise the days of small beginnings. David learnt how to fight while taking care of a few sheep; he stepped out in faith and killed the lion and the bear. One day, he found courage to step out in faith to kill Goliath.

When his confidence was in God, his confidence was not shaken by what others said. God remains the same. I loved it at the field, when his oldest brother ridiculed him, David didn't get offended

> They didn't expect much, so they didn't accomplish much.

and just moved on and killed Goliath.[23] He knew who he was. There had been speculations that he wasn't Jesse's legitimate son, which is why he was ostracised by his brothers. David didn't discount himself or feel inferior; he knew who he was in God.

So where do you put your confidence?

Antidote: Step out in faith

If you find yourself often feeling weak or despised by people around you, do not lose heart. You are a wonderful vessel for God to display His glory – if you put your confidence in Him! It's like a cracked pot; sometimes, the more cracked we are, the more light shines through us!

David would not have been able to step into his destiny as king of Israel if he were easily offended by people around him. He would not have been able to

---

23   1 Samuel 17

kill Goliath if he had not started shepherding his sheep faithfully. Faith is a muscle. Stepping out in boldness and trusting God is a muscle. Even confidence is a muscle. Keep showing up and confidence will turn up. We can develop these muscles as we take each step in obedience and watch God Himself train us and stretch us.

> Stepping out in boldness and trusting God is a muscle.

Then witness how He expands you. There are times, when you are tested to your breaking point, God takes over, breakthrough comes. The more you step out in faith, the more God-conscious you'll get, the less you'll be affected by what others say. The way of life indeed spirals upwards for the wise.[24] Choose to be wise.

> Keep showing up and confidence will turn up.

Activation:

Celebrate your weaknesses/failures. You can only get better! One day, you'll get to kill your Goliath!

Write down 3 things that you felt God wanted you to do but you have not done yet because of fear or

---

24   Proverbs 15:24 NKJV

feeling you are not up to it.

Then take action on them. Do not rationalise.

For me, it was writing. I had a dream to write in my teenage years, but because I failed my English, I ignored it. It was only when I turned 40, I promised myself to not refuse all that my heart tells me to do, as long as I can afford it and it's not against His will. By facing my greatest fear, I stepped into my destiny!

> By facing my greatest fear, I stepped into my destiny!

6. THE SIXTH SON: THE BULLY

The name of the sixth son of Haman is Aridatha. Its primary meaning is "the strong self," or, "self-assertive." Strong's Bible Dictionary translates this as "lion of the decree." This may mean overbearing or when aggressiveness gets out of control. It could reflect a stubbornness of going our own way without listening to counsel.

It could often happen to one when they've reached a certain level of success. There was a king called Asa. He started well; when he fought, he relied on

God and he won victoriously and received peace for many years. Towards the end of his reign, when war was pending, instead of seeking God and the counsel around him, he decided to go his own way and allied with others. When confronted, he was so angry that he placed his advisors in prison. He started well, but he did not end well; up to the very end, he chose not to seek counsel from his advisors nor from God.[25]

The beauty of being a strong-willed, stubborn, or assertive self is that when God calls this person, he can use his natural personality to be stubbornly single-minded for Christ!

Antidote: Seek advisors

If you find yourself having a strong-willed personality trait, congratulations, God can use you mightily – if you allow Him to guide you. Look at Paul; he was so strong-willed, assertive and a definite bully when he first went around persecuting the Christians. God met him in such a beautiful way that Paul spent the rest of his life being so focused to run his race. Being assertive is not a bad thing, as long as we are willing to allow God to guide and lead us into our destinies. We can then be His champions and run our race well!

---

25   2 Chronicles 16

Plans fail for lack of counsel, but with many advisers they succeed.

Proverbs 15:22 NIV

Surround yourself with mentors whom you can seek counsel from.

Be open to receive advice and rebukes. Be willing to be wrong. Ensure that they are mentors who have what you want in your life. We are not made to live life alone.

Why not seek someone who has gone ahead to help you shorten your journey?

Activation:

Reflect on the following and actively reach out:

Who are your mentors? You can have different mentors for different areas in your life. They can be people, programs or books. It is okay to invest in yourself! Spend money on your

> Surround yourself with mentors whom you can seek counsel from.

brain; it is retained. Spend money on food; it's flushed away in the drain! You are your greatest asset!! As Christians, we also have an advantage; we can also let the Word of God and the Holy Spirit be our guide! And They are free!!

For holistic clarity, I suggest the following 7 aspects for mentors. See if you can find mentors, books or programs in all these areas.

1. Spiritual
2. Emotional (the inner conditions of your heart)
3. Relational (your relationships e.g. marriage counselling)
4. Physical
5. Financial
6. Mental/Growth (depending on what you do)
7. Contribution

7. THE SEVENTH SON: THE NARCISSIST

Parmashta, the name of the seventh son means "preeminent self" or "self-ambition." When this is taken out of proportion, one will display Narcissist personality traits. In short, it means that one becomes selfish and overly concerned with themselves, needing excessive admiration and approval from others, while showing disregard for other people's sensitivities. If the narcissist does not receive the attention desired, substance abuse and major depressive disorder can develop.

There is a story in the Bible of a man who was talented from birth.[26] With his supernatural talents, he was meant to be set apart to steward what he carried. Before he was born, the angel of God met his parents and told them he was a special baby.

His name is Samson. He was gifted with supernatural strength. He knew he was special but unfortunately, he abused it. He used his strength to get what he wanted, including a woman who ultimately brought him to his downfall, going against his parents' advice.

He wanted to be the centre of attention and created such a havoc that his first wife and her family was burnt to death. He didn't learn from this and was still engrossed with his own needs. He found himself another woman who betrayed him. She knew his weakness. She knew if she gave him the attention he craved for, she could manipulate him. To his detriment, he was captured, his eyes were gouged out and he died very young.

The beauty of God's grace is that when God gifts

---

26   Judges 13 - 16

someone, this person will still accomplish His will, no matter how short-lived his life, and regardless of whether the motivation was pure. The person's obedience, however, determines the quality of the person's life. Samson died young, probably in his 30s; his success was short-lived but at the time of his death, he killed more of the enemies than in his lifetime.

> Don't ever let the desire for attention allow you to be manipulated and shorten your success.

The sad part is that if he had submitted to God and his parents right at the start, he could have used his strength to accomplish more and lived a lot longer. Don't ever let the desire for attention allow you to be manipulated and shorten your success.

Antidote: Rebuke such temptations and worship God!

If you find yourself talented and easily tempted for more power, first and foremost, I congratulate you that God has indeed placed a lot of talents in your life!! He has given you supernatural abilities like Samson that bring man's praise. Or maybe you actually have a heavenly assignment like Jesus, where the adversary will come and tempt you again and again for more power, for shortcuts, for you to have an inflated view of yourself.

If you would reject these temptations, submit and worship God, I'm believing that God will use you mightily above your human imagination. What you will step into, I guarantee you, will be much greater than what the devil promised you, because you have God on your side.

Jesus when tempted in the wilderness was approached by this same god of this world, but thankfully He overcame him.[27] He rebuked Satan and declared He would only worship God.

Thank God for the talents He has placed in you; don't ever hide them! That's false humility. Then, ask Him to enlarge your territory, as long as this ambition serves God's heart, which ultimately is people. Choose to add value to people, not to seek attention from them and watch Him bless your socks off!

Choose to add value to people, not to seek attention from them and watch Him bless your socks off!

---

27   Luke 4:5-7

Activation:

Thank God for your talents and worship Him! Go in the opposite spirit of a Narcissist!

As you worship Him, ask Him to show you His heart for the people around you or the people you manage. Learn to pray and bless people around you, to counter the tendency of elevating yourself.

Find a suitable community and be open to share your vulnerability. You don't have to be perfect to find acceptance; He is perfect and accepts you the way you are. Allow others to pray for you.

8. THE EIGHTH SON: THE STRIVING ONE

The eighth son is called Arisai and means "bold self" or "I am bold." We all need to be bold in what we do, but there is a point where it can go overboard. Without sufficient wisdom, our boldness can turn into striving or foolishness.

> A *prudent man foresees evil and hides himself,*
> But the simple pass on and are punished.
>
> Proverbs 22:3 NKJV

Boldness without discerning God's timing and without following what Jesus does can be devastating. Even though it may not sometimes make rational sense. It can also wound the soul with disappointments.

On the night when Jesus was betrayed, when the troops came to arrest Him, Jesus didn't run away; in fact, He said, "I am He." And then He said, "Let these go their way." He was willing to be captured and asked them to free his disciples. Peter, however, boldly attacked but was rebuked by Jesus.[28]

It made logical sense to protect Jesus. Peter instantly attacked the servant. He failed to listen to what Jesus said earlier, "Let these go their way."

If you read the entire account, the troops who came, initially fell at Jesus' feet, yet He had no intention to fight nor flee. Boldness is great, as long as we can quickly adapt to what Jesus is doing. It requires an alert mind, and more importantly, a heart after Him, an ear inclined to Him.

When we strive with our own efforts, we tend to run to the other extreme at the point of failure. Peter was bold and attacked the servant; in the next moment, he

28   John 18:8-11

retreated and pretended he didn't know Jesus. He was still relying on his own strength to protect himself. When the rooster crowed, he realised he had denied Jesus three times, just like what Jesus predicted; he was then so filled with condemnation that he ran away.

But the grace of God is so beautiful. Jesus prayed for Peter before he fell. He also restored Peter by lovingly speaking to Him one-on-one.[29] The angels specifically mentioned Peter's name to Mary at the tomb.

> *"... But go, tell His disciples—and Peter—that He is going before you into Galilee; there you will see Him, as He said to you."*
>
> *Mark 16:7 NKJV*

Antidote: Focus on Jesus, not your boldness

If you find yourself often caught in some rash bold activity, or you are struggling with condemnation of your mistakes, there is hope. God can gloriously redeem you for greatness just like how He used Peter mightily. Peter became the leader of all the other disciples because of his boldness. Peter learnt to

---

29   John 21

listen to Jesus and had a teachable heart.

There was only one disciple who remained at the cross when Jesus was crucified. Peter who claimed to be bold was not there. The rest of the disciples fled. This person was John. He was the one who professed he was Jesus' beloved.

Ironically, the boldest disciple was not one who boasted of himself, but the one who boasted of Jesus' love. He was the only brave one who remained. He knew God's heart. He didn't strive; he surrendered.

> Let your eyes be focused on Him who is constant rather than your own works.

Know that God desires your heart more than what you can do for Him. Let your eyes be focused on Him who is constant rather than your own works.

Activation:

Visualise or meditate how it would be to be like John, leaning on Jesus' chest. You'll get to feel His heartbeat, you'll get to feel how He feels.

Then ask God, "What is in Your heart?"

Pen down what comes to mind. Do not hold back.

9. THE NINTH SON: THE ARROGANT ONE

Aridai means "dignified self" or "I am superior." This can be seen as being proud or arrogant. There's a difference between confidence and arrogance. Beware of false humility as well! Some people who try too hard not to be arrogant but instead sounded weak. They end up displaying traits of the fifth son, the inferior one!

Confidence is an assurance of whose we are and who we are in God. That never changes, which allows our confidence to remain regardless of circumstances.

Arrogance is characterized by having an exaggerated sense of one's importance or abilities. Their identity is often tied to what they do or possess. When what they have or do is stripped away, they can enter the deepest and darkest depression, if they don't know their identity in God.

Most people don't start off arrogant, but as they receive successes along the way, they may become proud because of what they've accomplished. They forget it was God who blessed them. When someone is proud, he can also get judgemental and critical of others.

There are so many stories of defeated kings in the Bible; most of them started well, but sadly only 2 ended well. It's so easy to trust God and have a humble heart when you have nothing. But when God gives successes, the heart can so easily become proud.

> Confidence is an assurance of whose we are and who we are in God.

An example was King Uzziah. He became proud of himself and his accomplishments. He forgot it was God who granted him the victories in the first place!

> *But when Uzziah became strong, he became so proud [of himself and his accomplishments] that he acted corruptly, and he was unfaithful and sinned against the LORD his God.*
>
> *2 Chronicles 26:16a AMP*

The Bible does say that God opposes the proud and gives grace to the humble[30]. Hopefully we don't have to learn the hard way! Let us resolve in our hearts to end well and don't ever allow arrogance to creep in.

---

30   James 4:6

Antidote: Always give thanks

It is hard to be proud when you recognise that all you have is from God. Learn to give thanks for all the victories each day.

> *Oh, that men would give thanks to the Lord for His goodness,*
> *And for His wonderful works to the children of men!*
>
> *Psalm 107:31 NKJV*

Activation:

When we journal everyday what we are grateful for, we open our eyes to God's hands and favour in our lives. How can we be proud when we realise this?

Write down 5 to 10 things you are grateful for each day. This keeps our heart in a thankful posture. (There are many free mobile apps for a gratitude journal. I personally use "Presently" right before I sleep.)

10. THE TENTH SON: THE PHARISEE

The last name of the sons of Haman is Vaizatha, which means "pure self" or "self-righteous." It refers to those who consider that their acts attain their purity. Jesus was the harshest against the Pharisees and the Sadducees, despite their knowledge and legalistic practices. He calls them whitewashed tombs, beautiful outwardly but inside full of dead man's bones and all uncleanness. He said they appeared righteous to men, but were full of hypocrisy and lawlessness.[31]

I often wonder why Jesus was so direct and fierce to them! It must have been the one attitude He is against the most. If we look at the underlying motivation of the self-righteous, we can understand why.

Being legalistic or self-righteous, one looks at their own efforts, rather than God. One brings down the standard of purity to outward performances, not the inward heart posture and motivations. It's actually anti-Christ, proclaiming, "I don't need Jesus; I can attain salvation myself!"

Being legalistic or self-righteous, one looks at their own efforts, rather than God.

But who can judge the heart except God? A man can on the surface be loyal to his wife, but in his heart lust after another woman or lose the love he has for his

---

31   Matthew 23:27-28

wife. Or maybe simply he's just not attractive enough to woo other ladies, even if he wanted to! How can we tell? Leave all judgement to God.

> All a man's ways are pure in his own eyes, but his motives are weighed out by the LORD.
>
> Proverbs 16:2 BSB (Berean Study Bible)

God's standards are different. There is an account in the Bible of a rich young ruler who thought he had achieved everything. The very first question already reflected that he was focused on his own works, on what to "do."

Jesus immediately answered him, pointing him to the root of his issue. He said, "No one is good but One, that is God." He was telling the rich young ruler, "You will never be as good as God. No matter what you do, you'll always miss the mark.

> 17 Now as He was going out on the road, one came running, knelt before Him, and asked Him, "Good Teacher, what **shall I do** that I may inherit eternal life?"
>
> 18 So Jesus said to him, "Why do you call Me good? **No one is good but One, that**

is, God."

Mark 10:17-18 NKJV

The funny part about self-righteous people is that they have very low standards for themselves but harsh standards for others, leading to them judging and criticising others.

First, this rich young ruler professed that he has done everything God requires. Jesus looked at him and the Bible clearly says He loved him. He knew He came to die for this man who thought he can attain it himself. Jesus spoke the truth in love to pinpoint the motives of his heart. It wasn't that selling all that one has was the key to receive eternal life. He was revealing the young man's heart condition, that he loved his wealth and accomplishment more than God. That was a heart issue, not visible by what one does.

> *Then Jesus, looking at him,* **loved him**, *and said to him, "One thing you lack: Go your way, sell whatever you have and give to the poor, and you will have treasure in heaven; and come, take up the cross, and follow Me."*
>
> *But he was sad at this word, and went away*

sorrowful, for he had great possessions.

Mark 10:21-22 NKJV

Legalistic people also love to judge and condemn without careful self-examination first, which is a sin!!! The Bible tells us not to judge until we can see clearly, so that we ourselves are not judged.[32]

The reason why we need Jesus is that we are not perfect. No matter how much good we do, we cannot say that all our heart motivations are pure and are not for personal gain. In that light, we have all fallen and that is why Jesus came for us. That's the salvation story. It's not that we do good to get good. Rather, we first receive good to get good. We receive the good news of Jesus in our hearts and watch Him set us free emotionally, spiritually, and even physically, to be fully who He wants us to be.

> The reason why we need Jesus is that we are not perfect.

Stop examining yourself and getting into a self-condemning vicious cycle too. That's a religious act that still focuses on yourself, not God. Examine Jesus' finished work and allow the Holy Spirit to examine your heart and bring to light what you need to address. When Esther

---

32   Matt 7:1-5

went for her "beauty treatments", which represented purification, she didn't scrub herself! She allowed Hegai, representing our Lord Holy Spirit, to prescribe the beauty treatments, the scrubbing and purification. Trust our Lord Holy Spirit and yield to His leading and convictions.

Antidote: Remember His Finished Work on the Cross

If you are someone who has the tendency to be a perfectionist and evaluate your actions and condemn yourself or others, be kind to yourself and others. Remember it's not about you; it's about His finished work on the cross. Once you have believed and receive Jesus into your heart, then allow Him to lead you into all freedom. You do not need to do anything more to seek approval from God. A genuinely transformed life will result in good works. Know that you can find the freedom to live a pure and righteous life from a place of acceptance and approval. He has died on the cross for you; of course, He accepts you into His Kingdom!

Remember that at the Cross, all sins have been washed away: past, present, and future. Remember that the case is closed for others and for yourself, if you have received Jesus Christ in your heart.

> **So *now* the case is closed.** *There remains no accusing voice of condemnation against those who are joined in life-union with Jesus, the Anointed One.*
>
> *Romans 8:1 TPT*

It doesn't mean we don't lovingly correct, but we leave the judgement to God.

Activation:

No matter how outwardly good you are, imagine all your thoughts and imaginations are exposed for all to watch. Are you okay with that? Remember God's standard is not like ours!

At the cross, there is a divine exchange. Visualise the thief next to Jesus who entered Jesus' Kingdom, so we are not in a position to judge ourselves and others. Remember His grace.

Declare the case is closed in your life. Thank Jesus for the cross. Celebrate Him not your own works.

Declare that you are the righteousness of God in Christ.

6

ESTHER'S STRATEGIES

Esther has already decided to go to the king, but she didn't enter his court and petition immediately. A willing heart with a wrong method can often backfire. Imagine if Esther had stormed to the king right after; would it have worked? She didn't solely rely on her own boldness, but understanding the urgency, she gave herself 3 days to pray and seek God for strategies from above.

She sought divine help and wisdom that gave her divine favour; then she took action! Taking action is a sign of faith that you believe the strategy is from God.

There were 3 things she did that helped her win the victory.

1. COLLABORATION

It was exciting to watch how Mordecai and Esther worked together to achieve victory. It's a beautiful picture of how men and women can support each other to be both promoted to greater influence. We can achieve greatness for Him collectively when we work together, acknowledge and support each other wholeheartedly instead of striving.

> Men and women can support each other to be both promoted to greater influence.

Esther was wise enough to know that she cannot do it alone; hence, she asked Mordecai and the rest of the Jews to fast and pray. Fasting may appear like a waste of time, but it could turn things around. They fasted 3 days. Jesus was in the tomb for 3 days and on the last day He rose. He turned what was meant for evil to become a mighty victory. Esther learnt to trust in the supernatural God she served before she went about her tasks that seem so natural.

> Being spiritual, waiting on God's direction, does not mean being lazy.

She didn't just fast those 3 days; she also worked with the maids and prepared a banquet for the king at the same time. Our God is a practical God. Being spiritual, waiting on God's direction, does not mean being lazy. It requires us to take action in faith on what we believe He has deposited in our hearts.

We see in this story the beautiful unity and collaboration of the Jews. In times of turbulence, it is important that churches unite and rise up together, regardless of minor differences, to seek God for His wisdom in all things. Then we need to work together and put things in action.

Reflection:

Who are the Esthers in your life you can mentor? List 3 names.

Who are the Mordecais in your life who can mentor you? List 3 names.

Then be intentional to build these relationships and create structures, e.g. meeting your mentor once a fortnight or month.

2. COMMUNION

Esther put on her royal robes and came to the king boldly. The king already extended the scepter to her and said he would grant her anything. Esther did not ask the king to kill Haman straightaway. What was she up to?

She asked to dine with the king. She didn't even mention the matter the entire day. She wanted to spend time with him first. The way she petitioned to the king the next day, was very clever, "although the enemy could never compensate the king's loss.[33]" She chose to take time to know his heart and positioned her petition from his perspective. She was one smart woman!

When we pray, let us not only pray for what we want, but in accordance with His will. It requires intimacy, times of communion together to find out. If an earthly king extends his scepter, you know that our Heavenly King would do that too! Come boldly and be amazed by His favour, for He sees you beautiful. Esther had access to the inner court of the king; so do you. We now have direct access to our King for when Jesus died on the cross, the veil of the Holy of Holies was torn in two.[34]

Let us also feast before our King! Esther prepared a banquet, a feast. Our God is greater; He's already

---

33   Esther 7:4 NKJV

34   Mattjew 27:51

prepared the feast, in the presence of our enemies.[35] All we need to do is come.

The king mentioned it numerous times before Esther petitioned, "What do you want? It shall be granted, up to half my kingdom!" As you feast before our King, hear Him echoing the same thing, "What do you want, My bride?" Spend enough time to gain the boldness and confidence to ask all that you need!

> Esther had access to the inner court of the king; so do you.

As Esther came boldly, she stepped into her authority. She took back the signet ring from the enemy. She defeated the enemy and took back the authority.

As New Covenant Christians, we stand on the promise ground that Jesus had already defeated the greater Haman at the cross. When He was raised from the dead, He said, "All authority has been given to me in heaven and on earth.[36]" We now have every right to take back this signet ring. We can literally take communion of the bread (His body) and the wine (His blood) to remind ourselves of His finished work[37]. I

---

35   Psalm 23:5

36   Matthew 28:18

37   1 Cor 11:23

believe this is prophetic for what is happening in the world now. We too can come boldly to His Presence, to ask and take back the authority in ALL areas of our lives!

This could be an opportunity, despite the turbulent times, to experience the largest transfer of wealth and authority, as long as His sons and daughters rise up.

Let us come and feast before our King, in the presence of our enemies.

Reflection: Feast with your King

Take communion to remind yourself of the fact of Jesus' finished work. Thank Him.

When we feast together as a family, we can share with one another the good and bad of the day, with no other agenda except to enjoy one another's presence. Do the same with your King. Set up times to hang out with Jesus, regardless of your situation, in the presence of your enemy.

> Our God is greater; He's already prepared the feast, in the presence of our enemies.

How do you hang out with Jesus?

For me personally, I run on a very tight schedule with my commitments to write and to my family. When I first returned to Singapore, I struggled to find a quiet spot to seek Him. It was noisy everywhere! One day, I was walking near my office and sat on the swing while I was listening to His Word. I didn't even have to utter a word; I suddenly experienced this supernatural peace and a tangible presence of Him sitting next to me. I realised I don't have to travel far to hang out with Jesus! I felt as if God were saying, "Daughter, you got the order wrong. You are trying to still your heart before coming to Me. Peter walked on water **in** the storm. Come to Me that I may still your heart." Now I intentionally schedule breaks to take communion every day and to hang out with Him on this swing.

> Peter walked on water **in** the storm. Come to Me that I may still your heart.

Where can you hang out with Him? It won't be far, as long as you set the intention. It could even be when you are cooking! Hanging out with Jesus is as fun as playing on a swing. Let Him flood your soul with peace.

> Hanging out with Jesus is as fun as playing on a swing.

Then ask Him what does He say about you? Tell Him what's in your heart. Learn to celebrate, praise and worship, in the midst of your trouble.

3. CASTING YOUR CARES TO THE KING

After Esther had petitioned the king, things seem to go pear-shaped: the king left, she was left alone with the enemy standing across her! He even fell on her! But the king came back in time to save her.

> Trust our King to come and help us at the right time.

In the same way, trust our King to come and help us at the right time. I don't know why He likes to show up at the last minute, but I suppose it's a test of our faith, our belief that He will fight for us.

There was not even any record that Esther argued with Haman. **She simply remained seated.** That symbolises rest. She didn't fight Haman; she spoke to the king.

> She didn't fight Haman; she spoke to the king.

Esther had voiced out to the king; the rest of the battle belongs to him. She didn't have to worry. Too often in our prayers, we focus on the devil or our problems too much. Don't fight the devil; speak to our King; let Him fight for you. We too can resist the enemy by casting our cares on our King.

> *... casting all your care upon Him, for He cares for you. Be sober, be vigilant; because your adversary the devil walks about like a roaring lion, seeking whom he may devour.*

1 Peter 5:7–8 NKJV

Change your posture; remain seated and at rest. You don't even have to argue with the negative voices in your head. Just ignore them and speak to our King. Put your attention on Him who loves you, for He cares for you.

> Change your posture; remain seated and at rest.

Reflection:

What situation are you going through now?

How can you practically cast your cares onto Him and remain at rest?

7

TRANSFER OF AUTHORITY, INFLUENCE AND WEALTH

Finally, Haman was killed! He was hanged on the same gallows that he had initially created for Mordecai. What the enemy meant for evil, was turned around for good. Esther finally revealed her identity. She was given the house of Haman and Mordecai was given the signet ring, as a sign of authority of the king. The transfer of wealth[38] and authority had begun.

> See our King extending His scepter towards you, giving you the signet ring and His full authority.

But it's not over; it's just the beginning of the transfer of the authority. There was still a lot to be done.

The king had just helped Esther kill Haman; isn't it too much to ask the king of any other requests again? Esther boldly knelt before the king again, asking the king to revoke the evil scheme Haman had planned.

---

38   Proverbs 13:22

Again, the king held out the scepter to her.

Esther arose and stood before the king and asked for a new edict to be written. The king himself did not revoke Haman's evil edict; he told Esther and Mordecai to see to it. They were to write the decree as they pleased and to seal it with his signet ring. Esther and Mordecai set to work straightaway, releasing it within two months, to all the one hundred and twenty-seven provinces, to every people, in their own language. Esther did not just ask for protection; she proactively asked to annihilate the enemy!

See our King extending His scepter towards you, giving you the signet ring and His full authority. Not only does He favour you for protection and power, but He also favours you to uproot any enemy in your life. He will provide you all the resources to eliminate them. Yes, you can re-write your future, one that is full of hope and joy. Once you've sealed it with the signet ring, no one can revoke it.

We all now have been given authority through Jesus Christ in His name. I feel that God is saying, "I have given you all authority in heaven and on earth; now write the outcome you would like and walk in it." Esther and Mordecai wrote the decree as they deemed fit and acted on it.

There are some who are waiting on God for what to write, but God is waiting for us to pick up our authority and to act on it. I'm reminded of God and Adam in the garden. God asked Adam to name the animals. Imagine Adam asking back to God, "What shall I name them? Or "Lord, I'm waiting for you to give me a sign on what the name is." What would have happened? We may laugh about this, but a lot of Christians are waiting for God, when it is actually God who is waiting for them to act in faith and authority!

I love that Esther and Mordecai wrote messages to spread this good news so that it can reach all peoples, in their own language. The story revealed a great sense of urgency and they hastened to deliver the news.

Will you spread the good news of the gospel to as many around you as possible, with this same sense of urgency, so that more may rejoice?

When we rise up, we can excel in what we do, regardless of what others say. We can declare healing and wholeness in our lives. We can restore our wounded souls, so that we will prosper and be in health, just as our soul prospers.[39] We can make a difference, an impact, and occupy the different mountains of influence where He has placed us.

The book of Esther started with crying and mourning in the first month of the year, but it ended with joy and gladness, great victory and harvest in the final month of the year! Even though God was not mentioned, even though Esther and Mordecai were not in ministry positions, yet we know God was in it. Towards the end, people realised there was this invisible force resulting in many converting to Judaism. God will use you where you are, so that people around you can see the invisible force of Him in your life. Your testimony inspires them to put their trust in this invisible force too, this God.

Mordecai started out wearing sackcloth, but at the end, he was dressed in royal apparel. His apparel has hidden meaning too! He was symbolically clothed with the Holy Spirit, righteousness, kingship and royalty a representation of the bride of Christ.

Let us follow Esther's example to write and speak with full authority from our King. Let us communicate the good news like Esther and Mordecai, swiftly and with

___

39   3 John 1:2

a sense of urgency. Let us eradicate and uproot fully any hindrances that is in our hearts and in our way. Know that we have a decree issued from our King to do so.

I firmly believe that we have entered a new era, an Esther era where things will be different from before. In the past, we may have distinct positions. Some were kings, whom God sent to the marketplace. Some were priests, whom God appointed in the church and ministry.

If you notice in the book of Esther, there were no mention of priests. Esther and Mordecai were working for the king of Persia. Who were acting as the priests to remind others of God, to fast and to pray for deliverance? It was Esther. It was Mordecai. Most Bible studies also called them prophets.

> Let us follow Esther's example to write and speak with full authority from our King.

I believe in this new era, God will be raising up kings AND priests: people who excel in the marketplace and also birth His ministry, spreading His glory. It will be a season of supernatural favour and enablement, that one can do both assignments well. For years, there had been a misconception that priests must be poor. That's because we have not taken back the full authority! I declare priests in this new era will be effective kings in the marketplace too! It is time, time for us to arise, to reign on this earth.

> *"And have made us kings and priests to our God;*
> *And we shall reign on the earth."*
>
> *Revelation 5:10 NKJV*

If you are a home maker, feel empowered to not just raise up Kingdom children, but follow your heart to birth any ministries God has placed in your hearts. You may have to build your ministry as a business to sustain yourself. Why not? Church has been re-defined. So has ministry. It's no longer confined within the church hierarchy. I believe God is raising up men and women to birth ministries where they are, so that they can sustain themselves and minister to the people around them, in preparation for the harvest that's coming our way.

If you are in a corporate role, feel empowered to be a priest and minister to the people in the workplace. Perhaps God is asking you to address culture issues in the workplace by stepping up in leadership. Do that with the skills He has given you, coupled with the gifts of the Spirit. Be bold to pray for others when God leads you to. Or perhaps, you feel led to intercede specifically for your industry. Do so! Gather others to do so with you!

I'm believing we will also see successful Kingdom entrepreneurs, working professionals who have thriving business or corporate roles who will rise up to pastor, speak or lead in church in greater capacity too. Resources will no longer be an issue. When the world gets darker, His Church will shine brighter!

I'm believing we will see music, performing arts, media in the mainstream and leading the top charts in spiritual & new age genre, created by godly professionals to spread Kingdom values, His love and His supernatural healing peace. I believe we will see Holy Spirit pubs and bars so that we can be drunk with joy. I'm believing that God will place governmental leaders who will pray together, who will take on a prophetic role and anointing before they set the policies.

Be open to explore the different roles and dreams He has placed in your heart. God has uniquely positioned you where you are to fulfil the great commission. May God open your eyes to see your purpose in what you do.

And who knows but that you have come to your royal position for such a time as this? If you choose to arise, relief and deliverance will come. Yes, for the same God who helped Esther and Mordecai is with you.

I declare your time has come. Arise, shine, for your light has come! And the glory of the Lord is risen upon you. Yes, we may be in turbulent times, the darkness shall cover the earth, but the Lord will arise over you. His glory will be seen upon you and kings will come to the brightness of your rising[40].

> It is now time to arise,
> to be a star
> for His glory.

You shall not hide any longer. It is now time to arise, to be a star for His glory. It's not about you; it's about Him! May His name be glorified through you!

It is time to occupy, rule and reign in all mountains of influence – collectively as His bride. Let us write what we want to see and swiftly put that into action, in all languages throughout this earth.

---

40   Isaiah 60:1-3

He has positioned you to arise and witness the greatest

<blockquote>His Glory is already here.</blockquote>

transfer of authority, influence and wealth, and experience gladness, joy and honour like never before.

His Glory is already here.

Be found in the glory and shine.

Come, let us all arise!

Note:

Know that you are not arising alone, join the community on Facebook called, "The Arise Challenge". I'll see you there!

8

YOU CAN TOUCH THE SCEPTER ANYTIME

In the book of Esther, she had to risk her life to come to the king. She didn't know if the king would extend his scepter to her. She didn't know if he would favour her. Yet she went.

We now have a better deal in this New Covenant. We don't have to worry if the King will extend the scepter to us. This King of Kings wants us to come near so much that He has already extended the scepter.

> "I see Him, but not now; I behold Him, but not near; A Star shall come out of Jacob; **A Scepter shall rise out of Israel**, And batter the brow of Moab, And destroy all the sons of tumult.
>
> Numbers 24:17 NKJV

Jesus is our Scepter. **He has won us permanent favour.** Our Father wants you to come near so much that He sent His only beloved Son to where you are.

Jesus risked his life to be this Scepter. He came to earth so we can see Him, so we can come near and find favour. All we need to do now is arise, touch Him and receive all the favour we need.

> Jesus is our Scepter. **He has won us permanent favour.**

He is waiting.

Will you arise?

Come to Jesus to rule and reign in this life.

9

RECEIVE THIS KING

If you want to have this invisible force who grants supernatural favour in your life, know that He is already extending Himself towards you. His name is Jesus.

2000 years ago, a stronger Haman, the god of this world, Satan, was conquered when Jesus was hanged on the tree. That is our salvation story. That is our Jesus. He was the first one who arose and defeated the greater Haman by sacrificing His life – for you and me.

> *Christ has redeemed us from the curse*
> *of the law, having become a curse for us*
> *(for it is written, "Cursed is everyone who*
> *hangs on a tree"), ...*

Galatians 3:13 NKJV

If you still do not have a personal relationship with this King, know that He has already redeemed you from any curse that could have come upon you, and He wants to set you free and propel you into your destiny.

As a Christian, it doesn't mean we don't have troubles. It does mean that we have a God who will lead us forward. With Him by our side, we can turn things around. Personally, my main and foremost clarity is to know that He Himself will lead me in my next step. He who loves me will take care of me. I get to watch my life unfold to things I never thought or believed possible!

The Bible declares:

> *"For I know the plans I have for you"*, *declares the* LORD, *"plans to prosper you and not to harm you, plans to give you hope and a future."*
>
> Jeremiah 29:11 NIV
>
> *Jesus Himself said, "I have come that they may have life, and that they may have it more abundantly."*
>
> John 10:10b NKJV

The Bible says if you confess with your mouth and

believe in your heart that Jesus is Lord, He will come into your heart, save and guide you (Rom 10:9). If you want to do this, you can say the following prayer:

Dear Lord Jesus,

I confess that I do not want to live my life on my own. I need Your help. I confess I am imperfect, but You have overcome the curse of this world and You have set me free.

Because You chose to die on the cross for me, I trust that You will guide me into Your goodness and into the wonderful destiny and abundant life You have prepared for me.

I ask You to be my King, Lord Jesus. I repent of all my sins and turn from all wicked ways. I choose to go through the purification process by Your strength, Lord. I choose to arise with You and position myself to be a blessing. I declare I will learn to speak like royalty, to renew and transform my mind by Your Word for Your glory. I declare I will draw near to You for supernatural favour, to rule and reign in this life.

Thank You, Lord.

In Your name I pray, Amen.

Congratulations! You are now a believer in Jesus Christ. May I encourage you to continue reading the Bible, His Word, from the YouVersion Mobile App, attend a Jesus-loving church near you, and attend the Alpha series if the church organises it. I believe God will lead you to places you never felt possible. May the Bible verse below, one of my favourite verses, encourage you.

The Sovereign LORD is my strength;

he makes my feet like the feet of a deer;

he enables me to tread on the heights.

Habakkuk 3:19 NIV

10

PROPHECY FROM LANA VAWSER

This is a prophecy by Lana Vawser Ministries on 16 December 2020 that is aligned to the content of this book. The purpose is for these words to encourage you and for you to speak them over your life.

There is a declaration right after this, created for you to actively call forth this prophecy into fulfilment in your life.

For more prophecies, please refer to www.lanavawser. com

DAUGHTERS OF GOD, RECEIVE YOUR PROMISE

Recently I heard the Lord say, "Daughters of God, RECEIVE YOUR PROMISE" and I saw daughters of God all over the world and they have been hearing the Lord say, "NOW IS THE TIME FOR THE MANIFESTATION OF THE PROMISE." They continue to hear the Lord speaking those words over and over "NOW IS THE TIME." They have waited and they have believed. I heard Luke 1:45 "Blessed is she who has believed that there would be a fulfilment of what was spoken to her from the Lord."

I began to see daughters of God all over the world beginning to receive the manifestation of that which the Lord has spoken to them. They were moving from hope deferred to hope assured. They were moving from discouragement to joy. From despair to dreaming again. The Lord is breathing refreshing hope and life over many daughters right now. The long-awaited promises are manifesting now. I heard many daughters of God crying out, "I have waited my whole life for this." The faithfulness of God resounded loudly around me as I watched daughters of God falling on their knees weeping and weeping in joy and thankfulness to the Lord that He has fulfilled that which He has spoken and that which He had promised.

Isaiah 66:9 surrounded me:

'Shall I bring to the time of birth, and not cause delivery?" says the Lord; "Shall, I who cause delivery shut up the womb?" says your God.

Daughters of God, the time has arrived for you to see the GOD WHO DELIVERS bring forth delivery in a way you have NEVER SEEN before. The mighty powerful hand of God is going to bring forth that which He has spoken to you. He is going to deliver it, He is going to sustain it, He is going to watch over it, and He is going to cause it to flourish.

This mighty demonstration of God's hand to bring forth DELIVERY is not only bringing forth the manifestation of that which He has spoken, but I see the manifestation of that which He has spoken manifesting in your life being such a testimony of His goodness, His kindness, and faithfulness to you, that hearts are going to be healed.

I saw so many of the hearts of His daughters that were battle-weary, bruised from the battles, tired, discouraged, and broken, the Lord is healing hearts.

The manifestation of the promise will testify to His goodness and His kindness that is above and beyond what you have imagined, the revelation of His nature and His faithfulness to do what He said He will do is going to heal your heart by the power of His Spirit.

The Lord showed me that many daughters of God have waited what feels like their whole lives for this moment. There is such a significant breaking forth that is going to take place in the delivery of His promises right now, that is going to cause them to fall even deeper in love with Jesus. I saw hearts going from dry, tired, and discouraged suddenly into a level of encounter with Him and His love that simply has not been walked in or experienced before. The depth of intimacy I saw taking place between the daughters of God and their Beloved I don't have adequate words to articulate. The manifestation of receiving these promises and the revelation of His nature will be so profound it is going to change everything and cause deep transformation of the heart for many daughters of God.

The Lord spoke to me about a new land of inheritance for the faithful daughters of God. The Lord spoke again, "To those who have overcome, inherit your land of promise." There was such a strong sense that surrounded me again of Luke 1:45 and blessed is she who has believed that there would be a fulfilment of what the Lord spoke. The Lord continued to speak, "This is not a false start. This manifestation of My promise to you will not be shaken, it will not be stolen, it will not be stalled. My faithfulness carries this promise, and it is time for delivery. For in this new land of inheritance you will find great joy. You will experience a realm of joy in Me that you have not known before. The joy will spring up from within you and bubble out from every part of you as your heart rejoices and sings "MY GOD IS FAITHFUL." This deeper level of joy that you are entering into is found in the revelation of My nature. For many of you, My daughters, you have waded through waters of disappointment, you have walked through the valleys of despair, you have battled over the giants of fear and intimidation all over this promise that has been weighing on your heart, well now in this new land of receiving that which I have spoken, moving into a new land of inheritance, your heart shall rejoice like you have never rejoiced before, you will move into a deeper level of intimacy with Me and praise of My name as you see just how good I am and how faithful I am to accomplish that which I have spoken."

PROVERBS 17:22

I heard Proverbs 17:22 resounding:

"A joyful heart is good medicine, but a broken spirit drains one's strength." (ISV)

"A joyful, cheerful heart brings healing to both body and soul." (TPT)

The Lord showed me that not only will the manifestation and receiving of the promise not only cause the daughters of God to fall even more deeply in love with Jesus and bring healing to hearts, but the Lord also showed me the explosion of joy in the revelation of His faithfulness and His nature and walking in the promise will fill the heart with SO much joy that many bodies will SUDDENLY be healed, and youth will be renewed. I saw that many daughters of God had become 'heartbroken' and 'heartsick' in the battle that has taken place over the promise, some for years, others for decades, and the heart was sick with trauma, pain, and hope deferred and it had caused many physical issues and ailments within bodies, but our beautiful Jesus by His Spirit is setting many daughters free not only of hope deferred, pain and trauma but also of many years of debilitating cycles of sickness and disease that was springing forth from the DIS-EASED heart.

I hear the Spirit of God speaking over the daughters of God, "It's time to breathe again in a deeper revelation of who I am and My love. It's time for a deep, unprecedented, never visited before place of the Song of Songs divine dance with Me. Here you come, My beautiful daughter, coming up out of the wilderness leaning upon Me. Empowered. Healed. Set Free and having received the promise of that which I had spoken. For many of you, My daughters, it is time for you to learn what it is to TRULY LIVE AGAIN! From surviving to thriving. This is the season you have been waiting for. It's time to FLOURISH!"

DECLARATIONS

I am the daughter of the Most High God.

This is the year for the manifestation of God's promise.

God will deliver all He has put in my heart.

I receive all kindness and goodness from God.

I receive revelation of His nature and faithfulness.

I received a healed heart by the power of the Holy Spirit.

I declare breakthrough this year.

I declare that God will bring me into a new land of inheritance.

I declare I am an overcomer.

I declare that I receive joy and it will bubble out from every part of me.

I receive physical and emotional healing in every part of me.

I receive supernatural youth and vitality.

I enter into deeper intimacy with God.

I dance with Jesus.

I lean on Jesus, empowered, healed and free!

I declare this is the year I will flourish!

MESSAGE FROM THE AUTHOR, RUTH SAW

I hope this book has been helpful for you. Please help me by placing a review on Amazon or Goodreads. It will help encourage other ladies to read this book!

Please also share this book with as many female friends as you have and invite them to the FB community. Help me in my mission to gather women to arise!

Note: Know that you are not arising alone, join me in the Facebook group where there will be additional video teachings on how you too can find the clarity to arise.

You can look for the Facebook group, "The ARISE Challenge" or scan the QR Code to join.

ABOUT THE AUTHOR

Ruth Saw (MBA) is an international bestselling author, speaker, and a clarity expert. As a Gallup certified strengths coach and having been trained in bible college including YWAM, she now helps others step into their God-given destinies, through books, coaching, and workshops.

Having lived and worked in different cultures, including the United States of America and Asia Pacific in her consulting practice and corporate career in procurement, she realises that regardless of culture, people will flourish when they know who they are, when they find clarity.

Now Ruth utilises her corporate and coaching experience to enhance organisational and individuals' performance. Through unpacking the strengths of a leader or a team, she helps individuals, organisations and start-ups find their clarity and maximise their performance, just the way they are.

She herself, found clarity and freedom in pursuing her passion (despite being an introvert!) and now she's dedicated to helping others find their clarity.

ACKNOWLEDGEMENTS

A big thank you to the following for believing in me and helping me to bring this book to life. There are so many people who have helped me in this journey. If your name is not listed, you know I appreciate you too.

- Dr. Jen Miskov & SOR Family – for being my family, for encouraging me and for helping me birth this book to life.

- L.M. McCormick – thank you for allowing me to reference and adapt your works into this book. You are a confirmation for me to write this book!

- Kevin & Lana Vawser – for your prophecies that changed my life, for your encouragement and teaching me how to be a friend of Jesus.

- Ana Werner – for your encouragement and for sharing the exact theme verse of the book that brought me confirmation to write it!

- Daryl Crawford – for providing me clarity and words of confirmation.

- Johnny & Liz Enlow – for your teaching of the 7 mountains and reminding us to conquer every sphere.

- Comfort Olutola & Aja McCombs – for your constant prayers and encouragement.

- 100X Acceleration Family - for your training, prayers and support.

- Lorellee & Phil Colley - for speaking words of encouragement over my life.

- Ching, Naomi Deck & Debbie Wong - for your constant prayers, support and friendship.

- My brother David Saw & Linda Beaulieu - for the detailed editing and proofreading of this book.

- Deasy and Seya - for the beautiful book cover.

- Deasy - for the immaculate layout, illustrations and typesetting of the book.

- My outstanding launch team, friends and family - for your support to launch this book!

Most importantly, I give all praise and glory to my King and Giver of good gifts—my Father in heaven, my Lord Jesus, my Refiner's fire, Lord Holy Spirit. Thank

You for guiding and helping me throughout the entire process to create and birth forth this book. I love You because You first loved me. Thank You for extending the scepter towards me and for loving me.

MORE INFORMATION ABOUT TCE'S BOOKS, WORKSHOPS AND AUTHORISED ONLINE PROGRAMS.

ABOUT THE PUBLISHER
THE **CLARITY** EXPERT

The Clarity Expert (TCE), founded by Ruth Saw, is a faith-based publisher that aims to shine Christ's brightness, radiance, glory and splendour through stories.

TCE's mission is to make all spiritual language plain, so that this power can be made accessible to all men and women.

TCE believes that true clarity comes from above and seeks to offer authentic and true testimonies to encourage, inspire and motivate. TCE also believes that God can do great things through ordinary, broken men and women, when we allow Him to lead and guide.

> *"Very truly I tell you, whoever believes in Me will do the works I have been doing, and they will do even greater things than these, because I am going to the Father. And I will do whatever you ask in My*

name, so that the Father may be glorified in the Son. I will ask the Father, and He will give you another Advocate to help you and be with you forever."

John 14:12-14, 16 NIV

ABOUT CLARITY IS POWER

CLARITY IS POWER.

"Just like a diamond, the more clarity we have, the more value we bring." Ruth Saw

Clarity unlocks not only the why, it points us to the how. When we know who we are, we find freedom from comparing ourselves with others. We will step up into our personal authority with strength and confidence to be the best version of who we can be, for ourselves and for those around us.

In this book, Ruth uncovers practical steps to finding clarity using easy-to-understand stories, as well as simple exercises.

Read the book to find your personal clarity, for you to move past your doubts and step into your destiny!

Clarity is power.

And that power is YOU!

Available on major bookstores such as AMAZON, KOBO, Barnes & Noble, Book Depository and major bookstores in Singapore and Malaysia.

A signed copy is available for deliveries in Singapore.

To purchase, visit: www.theclarityexpert.co

ABOUT CLARITY TO CREATE

JESUS IS CALLING. "Dance with Me, My love. Allow Me to lead, let Me take you to places you've never been."

You are more powerful than you think. Every woman is born to create. By experiencing perfect love and union from above, you can birth forth dreams that could change you and the world. It is time for all women to rise up to our God-given destinies.

You will learn 5 simple keys to create, using inspiring stories of women in the Bible, as well as simple and practical exercises that will expand not only your vision and your destiny but also your heart.

If you feel that there is more to your destiny, then this book is for you.

Your dreams matter.

You matter.

He loves you.

Available on major bookstores such as AMAZON, KOBO, Barnes & Noble, Book Depository and major bookstores in Singapore and Malaysia.

A signed copy is available for deliveries in Singapore.

To purchase, visit: www.theclarityexpert.co

DISCLAIMER

The material in this publication is for general comment only and does not represent professional advice. It is not intended to provide specific guidance for particular circumstances, and it should not be relied on as a basis for any decision to take action or not take action on any matter which it covers. Readers should obtain professional advice where appropriate, before making such decision. To the maximum extent permitted by law, the author and publisher disclaim all responsibility and liability to any person, arising directly or indirectly from any person taking or not taking action based on the information in this publication.

TRAINING PROGRAMS

If you would like to take it further, you can sign up for available training courses for a guided experience into finding your clarity.

BE UNIQUELY YOU

Helping you to be uncover the gold within and shine

This is an interactive "Find Your Clarity" workshop and group coaching where you will uncover the gold in you and find out how uniquely wired you are! You will get to unpack your strengths and learn a strengths-based approach to create the strategies you need to be a better you. It also involves developing a personalised action plan that will cause you to shine holistically.

BREAK YOUR LIMITING BELIEFS

Helping you to remove all that hinders and fly

This is an interactive "Find Your Clarity" workshop and group coaching where you will identify the limiting beliefs and labels that have hindered you. You will find the clarity to break those lies and find the freedom to be who you are meant to be. The course is intensive, and participants must commit to attending the entire course for maximum results.

CLARITY TO WRITE ONLINE COURSE

Helping Authors to Rise - AuthorRise Program & Coaching

This is a comprehensive step-by-step online program from writing to publishing your book and becoming a best-selling author. It includes worksheets, exercises and links to free and affordable resources to empower you, find success and get your story out!

There is also an option for live group coaching and mentoring to fast-track your success.

To find out more or register your interest, and to be included in the mailing list, please see link below or scan the QR code:

https://www.theclarityexpert.co/training-programs

Printed in Dunstable, United Kingdom

85224507R00107